BLESSED

Blessed

GOD'S GIFT OF LOVE

ברך

Mary J. Moerbe

with Christopher Mitchell

CONCORDIA PUBLISHING HOUSE · SAINT LOUIS

Published by Concordia Publishing House
3558 S. Jefferson Ave., St. Louis, MO 63118-3968
1-800-325-3040 • www.cph.org

Manufactured in the United States of America

Library of Congress Cataloging-in-Publication Data

Moerbe, Mary J., 1980- author.

Blessed : God's gift of love / Mary J. Moerbe, with Christopher W. Mitchell.

St. Louis: Concordia Publishing House, 2016. | Includes bibliographical references.

LCCN 2015049728 (print) | LCCN 2016007911 (ebook) | ISBN 9780758651822 | ISBN 9780758651839 ()

LCSH: Blessing and cursing in the Bible. | Blessing and cursing. | God (Christianity)--Love.

LCC BS1199.B5 M64 2016 (print) | LCC BS1199.B5 (ebook) | DDC 264/.1--dc23

LC record available at http://lccn.loc.gov/2015049728

1 2 3 4 5 6 7 8 9 10 25 24 23 22 21 20 19 18 17 16

In thanks to God for my double portion of blessing,
Anastasia and Dorothea.
MJM

Table of Contents

Acknowledgments

This book would not have been possible without the careful and extensive scholarship of my coauthor, Dr. Christopher Mitchell. His dissertation, *The Meaning of* BRK *"To Bless" in the Old Testament,* published by Scholars Press (Atlanta), copyrighted in 1987 by the Society of Biblical Literature, offers both careful research and many eureka moments.

Thank you to my family: my husband, who supported me and allowed me the necessary time; my mother, who kindly assisted in whatever ways she could; and my dear children, who happily bonded with their grandmother. Special thanks also to Holly Scheer, who offered valuable insight and feedback along the way.

Thank you to the pastors in my life, including but not limited to my beloved husband, Rev. Ned A. Moerbe, Rev. James Douthwaite, Rev. Adam Hensley, and many more.

MJM

Introduction

God bless you!" is said because someone's suffered loss: a relationship, a job, or a loved one. Or, "Bless you!" when the person before you has made a positive difference in someone's life. "Bless you" ends an email and graces a greeting card. "Bless you!" simply because someone sneezed! Adding together scenarios, blessings can be common, everyday occurrences.

On the other hand, *blessing* can be a foreign word and concept. What does it even mean? How in the world would a word of blessing affect your after-sneeze?

Do blessings affect days and weeks, let alone sicknesses, marriages, pregnancies and babies, and other Hallmark moments? In times of fear, suffering, or loss, can a few words and well-wishes really make a difference? Are blessings more than words? Should they be sought? What about things people call blessings that don't initially seem like blessings? The questions go on, as do the scenarios that conjure them.

When Martin Luther was hidden away in Wartburg Castle, living each day as though it might be his last, he translated the Bible into German. He later spoke about trembling before each letter, as God is in every syllable![1] And before us now is an opportunity to consider blessings, a concept our Lord spells out by His Word.

Blessing is a weightier word than many and a concept worthy of our consideration. It is a concept given to us by God and revealed in His Word. It is both common and spectacular—and its spectacle is Christ Jesus, our Lord, who suffered, died, and was buried before He rose again, ascended into heaven, and now sits at the right hand of God, the Father Almighty.

Even so, *blessing* is a word Christian children absorb into their vocabulary often with little explanation. They hear and gather together the different contexts—from sneezes to well-wishes to wanting to be blessed by God—and gradually mimic them appropriately. They quickly learn that blessings are good and that God is the great source of blessings.

This is a profound confession of faith! May God's littlest children remind us of that often, because even that basic sentiment can slip away from those older and considered wiser.

God is the giver of every good and perfect gift, a revelation from God Himself (James 1:17). We do not grasp the revelation naturally; it is taught to us. Or, to put it another way, it is given to us. Gift after gift forms a chain of unbroken love by the infinite giver.

As children grow, they typically add nuances to their understanding of terms and concepts. Even foreign words become second nature—can I hear an *alleluia*? Sometimes, though, words get overlooked. Lessons get lost. Time slips away, and memories are forgotten.

We can admit that a lot of adults would stumble too if suddenly asked what makes something a blessing or a person blessed, especially when blessings so often develop differently than we expect. Hard times come, and it takes faith to see beyond our struggles.

This can affect us all. We may "ask a blessing" at mealtimes, but not really consider why we ask for bread to be blessed. We are explicitly blessed by the Benediction in a worship service, but may not think about it very much—many having been blessed since childhood. What is happening in those times and places? How do we answer the Church's call to "Bless the Lord"?

Let us say we have forgotten. We forget all the time. We forget lyrics to our favorite songs, and we get reintroduced to the most famous and powerful story of all times on a constant basis. This is just one of many reasons why we should keep reading and studying Scripture. Under normal circumstances, our human ears hold only so much for so long.

Scripture reveals blessings. It answers our questions about what it means, what it looks like, who gets what, and who favors whom. Blessing is a common and integral theme throughout Scripture. It includes incredibly important stuff! At the same time, though, it reveals smaller gestures and habits too. The blessings our Lord reveals in Scripture can be timeless or temporal gifts, showing love and mercy to His creation.

Blessings predate understanding. Before we understand what

blessing means in our own lives, we may already have the greatest, everlasting one: Jesus as Savior. All because it is God who blesses, and He does so freely for the sake of His Son, working through His Word even for those at the most tender ages.

The father of lies, however, is true to his name. He lies about blessings. He seems to particularly love twisting God's good gifts and distorting God's Word. Therefore, He often has twice the incentive to lie about blessings, which are both signs and expressions of God's grace.

The devil likes to lie about curses too. He is the accuser (Zechariah 3:1). He prefers to relive the trial than to admit the eternal Judge's verdict (Revelation 12:10–11). But condemned and caged, our adversary the devil still "prowls around like a roaring lion, seeking someone to devour" (1 Peter 5:8). He likes to nibble away at anything that comes too close to him, including language and phrases God gave us for our instruction and good.

Relying on human instinct or common language is not sufficient to come to a Spirit-led understanding of blessings. Christian lessons about blessings must be revealed. By God's Word and working of the Spirit, God must reveal Himself and His gifts.

Blessings are an expression and gift, given and enacted by God for His creation and those in His favor. Blessings can be spoken, prayed, wished, and embodied. In the hands of the Creator, they can be an intimate expression of the potential good in the world. In the hands of infinite Love, they are part of the boundless, steadfast mercy of the triune God.

There are so many examples and lessons in Scripture: God's blessing of the animals and man in creation; the blessings of the patriarchs Abraham, Isaac, and Jacob; the Covenantal Blessings for Israel; blessings in Wisdom Literature; Apocalyptic Blessings; benedictions; and more. And that list is limited to the Old Testament! The Beatitudes are eight blessings listed in the Sermon on the Mount (Matthew 5), though the epitome of blessing in Scripture, of course, is Jesus Himself, sent by His Father and filled with the Spirit.

Scripture revolves around God as He blesses, but people bless throughout Scripture too. There are prayers to bless others, priestly rituals, and greetings. There were blessings of thanksgiving, especially at such momentous events as births, weddings, deaths, and so on. And, in addition to man blessing man, there is also man blessing God.

This book will explore blessings by the work of the Holy Spirit in the grounding of God's Word. We will focus on the Hebrew root *brk* (most commonly pronounced *berak*) as used in the Old Testament. While various forms of the English term *blessing* can be found in nearly 500 places throughout Scripture, *brk* appears 402 times in the Old Testament! The root is so common that there are specialized formulaic uses particularly necessary for translators to understand, though this work will not address all of those.

Rev. Dr. Christopher Mitchell, however, took the time to catalog and analyze the use of the Hebrew terminology of "blessing" (the verb *berak* and noun *berakah*) throughout the entire Old Testament. His previous work, published under the title *The Meaning of* BRK *"To Bless" in the Old Testament* (Scholars Press, 1987), includes a complete study of the Hebrew term. So, although some technical translation notes go beyond the breadth of this book, he clarifies many misunderstandings and grammatical mysteries in that previous work.

We will see archetypes—defining symbols and motifs—as well as the common graces with which God blesses creation in general. We will see specific blessings to individuals and corporate blessings for countries and faith communities. All this is not to advance abstract knowledge of history, but to lend insight into salvation and God Himself. Learning about blessing adds depth to our understanding of Him who blesses.

Christians worship the Word made flesh and the God who spoke creation into being. We speak of the faith that comes from hearing (Romans 10:17) and the words of eternal life (John 6:68). May we always take interest in God's words!

MJM

CHAPTER 1

Misconceptions

Greetings cards are on to something by offering sweet sentiments of hope and joy at special times. Weddings are beautiful because God Himself crafts every married man into one flesh with his married woman. Births are a fantastic celebration of life and new beginnings! Sickness can encourage help and compassion, and every thank-you note acknowledges another person in thought, word, and deed.

Cards can commemorate blessings, and that is a worthwhile thing to do. At the same time, not everything celebrated is truly a blessing. As individuals seek acceptance within society, they may seek a blessing from the world that actually defies God.

As a word, blessing can have a broad and a narrow sense. Broadly, one could say just about everything is a blessing, understanding blessing in terms of a gift or good thing. More narrowly, however, the Bible portrays blessings as a gift from *God*. In fact, a blessing is not only a gift but an expression or act of God's goodwill and favor toward the recipient. It originates with God. It is accomplished by God and accompanied by Him.

> Blessings are a gift *from God*
> that originate with God and are both
> accomplished and accompanied by Him.

The broad sense has its places. Can a parking spot be a blessing from God? The Bible has not said so. Still, one spot made handicapped may suddenly allow a person to attend church and receive the gift of life everlasting. That is not a coincidence slipping past the Almighty's notice. It is a gift to those who benefit from it. Or even a free spot that allows you to make that interview on time. God works in mysterious, but sometimes simple, ways.

Still, it does not necessarily follow that the person who cut you off to grab a good parking spot is more favored by God than you, who had to walk a distance. Nor is lack of parking divine punishment upon you. People sometimes think that way, about red lights or things much more serious: "Her cancer is in remission, but mine isn't. God, what are You trying to tell me?"

Although it is a natural response for individuals to look for signs and explanations in this life, especially in times of need or upheaval, God graciously uses the words of Scripture to reveal His will. Blessed gifts support that revelation, although sometimes in ways we cannot understand. Many things we accept "by faith, not by sight" (2 Corinthians 5:7), because we must trust God's Word.

Let us be clear and upfront. Luke 13 is clear that tragedy and disaster is not a divine revelation that those who suffer are worse sinners (Luke 13:1–5), and death spreads to all men (Romans 5:12). Scripture does not direct us to omens, horoscopes, and daily signs. Instead, again and again, we are pointed to God's Word and Jesus Christ.

From a young age, King David knew distrust and betrayal. He was experienced in war and bloodshed. He saw sin and abuse within his family, and he knew firsthand man's dire need for a savior. From the darkness of the fallen world, he prayed, "Show me a sign of Your favor . . . because You, LORD, have helped me and comforted me" (Psalm 86:17).

No matter how much we might be tempted to read into Scripture, blessings are not a reflection of how well we are doing in this life. Blessings are not about *us*; rather, blessings are about *God* who gives them. Blessings are exactly what King David asked for: a sign of God's merciful favor.

We may receive cards, notes, or messages from our friends, but our Lord sent His Son and His Word to us. His Son enters our suffering and grief.

Jesus answers our needs and prayers, even as He turned and was gracious to David, giving "strength to Your servant . . . the son of Your maidservant" (Psalm 86:16). He incorporates us into Himself so that, in Him, we will be forever blessed. The Old Testament tokens and signs of affection come together in Jesus to such a glorious extent that, when we want to see blessing, we may look directly to Christ Himself.

Fears and Distress

Sadly, most do not consider Jesus part of the equation, let alone an eternal fulfillment, of God's blessing. Life is hard. We suffer. Some may feel unworthy or left out. Some may see themselves as plagued by bad luck. Others may tremble because they consider themselves unchosen, even by God.

All of these fears can be shaped by our perception of blessings. Will blessings ease my suffering? Will they come to help? What do I need to do? Do blessings come only to the worthy? Will I be passed by and forgotten? What if I get more than I can handle?

Blessings exist on an extremely wide spectrum. On one side, blessings seem like mere perks. On the other, a fistful of bread saves a life. The middle can hear "Bless you" as an offhanded comment falling short of a minimal prayer. Some absolutely fear blessings, while others fail to recognize what they are.

There are Christians right now questioning whether God will ever bless them, feeling as devastated as a psalmist![1] Good can seem so temporary, while harm seems so resolute. Enemies rise up. Help feels fleeting, while problems are unmovable.

If you are watching something good suddenly dissolve and disappear, or if you are experiencing loss or uncertainty right now, Christ is still interceding *that you be blessed* by the "God and Father of our Lord Jesus Christ, who has blessed us in Christ with every spiritual blessing in the heavenly places, even as He chose us in Him before the foundation of the world, that we should be holy and blameless before Him" (Ephesians 1:3–4).

Every spiritual blessing in the heavenly places does not mean we are comfortable now. The apostles certainly were not comfortable then! Romans 8:18–26 describes the sufferings of this time as creation groaning, believers groaning, and the Holy Spirit groaning! The world can be confounding on every imaginable level, but Christ is coming to rescue, restore, and resurrect. Because of Him, God looks upon us with favor.

Some hear the message that, because God blesses those faithful to Him, Christian life is supposed to be easier than non-Christian life. Such misconceptions can color how we understand Scripture, how we see ourselves, and how we relate to one another. "Your baby is healthy! You are so blessed!" "God has blessed your prayers! Your cancer is in remission!" But when a person believes that blessings are given to the healthy and whole, what of the sick or broken? If blessings are for the successful, what of the struggling or failed? What of those with no help? What of addicts and those without self-control?

Comforts can be treated as a divider against those in need of comforting! Such a misunderstanding of blessing turns away from faith. It emphasizes circumstance and suffering rather than Christ and His objective Word.

The subjective nature of perspective sadly can inhibit one's reading of Scripture and reception of comfort. And by unintentionally conjuring one's own assumptions, desires, emotions, and fears into the religious life, the individual may even question whether he or she has faith.

With many thanks to God, even if faith were lost, "faith comes from hearing, and hearing through the word of Christ" (Romans 10:17). To whom shall we go? Christ has the words of eternal life (John 6:68).

Instead of an us versus them dichotomy between the blessed and the wretched, the apostle Paul reminds us:

> For we ourselves were once foolish, disobedient, led astray, slaves to various passions and pleasures, passing our days in malice and envy, hated by others and hating one another. But when the goodness and loving kindness of God our Savior appeared, He saved us, not because of works done by us in righteousness, but according to His own mercy, by the washing of regeneration and renewal of the Holy Spirit, whom He poured out on us richly through

> Jesus Christ our Savior, so that being justified by His grace we might become heirs according to the hope of eternal life. The saying is trustworthy, and I want you to insist on these things, so that those who have believed in God may be careful to devote themselves to good works. These things are excellent and profitable for people. (Titus 3:3–8)

The blessed still need the good works of others in this fallen world. There can be blessing in the midst of pain and anguish. There is hope despite extreme need. There is love in spite of the world of hatred, violence, and greed. The triune God sows these good things generously, even among the thorns and crosses, knowing He can cover greater ground than all sin, death, and power of the devil.

When the rain falls and the floods come and the winds blow, how do you know whether you built your house upon the sand (Matthew 7:24–27)? We may not understand why the Lord allows certain things, but we can remember that rain, floods, winds, and storms come to us all, the wise and foolish alike. And whether Christ calms the storm or not, He is with us always, even to the end of the age (Matthew 28:20).

Cards can offer support, approval, and even a wished blessing. They can be a tangible sign and expression of your own affection, but blessings in the hands of our incarnate God are much deeper than cardstock and address a broader range of realities than even the broadest assumptions. A card may wish you smooth transitions and an easy time in a religious-sounding way. Blessing from God, however, carries through the darkest days too.

The Beatitudes in Matthew 5 and Luke 6 turn many assumptions about blessings upside down. Blessed are the poor, the hungry, and those who weep, says our blessed—and blessing—Lord, who Himself became poor. He hungered, wept, was tortured, and died for our sake, that we may receive the heavenly Father's good favor.

Temptations

While blessings are something we can pursue, they are never a reason to covet. In fact, there is no reason to covet, because God has promised to provide. He has promised daily bread, yet feeds you with Bread from heaven. He is mindful of you now (Psalm 8:3–5) and into eternity (John 4:14).

The Bible tells us that the disciples, at times, fought among themselves, comparing themselves and what Jesus said of them. But when the apostles were concerned with their standing and future, Jesus calmly asked, "If it is My will that he remain until I come, what is that to you?" (John 21:23).

God has not promised to provide everyone with the same things, or in the same ways, and we have the example of the disciples and countless others in Scripture to assure us that, despite our fears—and the truly dreadful things that can happen in this life—the triune God keeps His promises. In Scripture, we see how God's blessings unfold within time, come to us now, and carry us into the age to come, which has no end.

Yet so often, when confronted with God's Law, we gird our loins and think, This time I will be better. This time I will be deserving. However, a large point in Scripture is that we are saved *by Jesus* and not by *deserving* at all. This pertains to blessing, because many assume that blessings must always be gained by a pure heart or earned by works—by personal strengths.

Consider this text from the apostle Paul:

> [The Lord] said to me, "My grace is sufficient for you, for My power is made perfect in weakness." Therefore I will boast all the more gladly of my weaknesses, so that the power of Christ may rest upon me. For the sake of Christ, then, I am content with weaknesses, insults, hardships, persecutions, and calamities. For when I am weak, then I am strong. (2 Corinthians 12:9–10)

Looks can be deceiving. We look around and see earthquakes, tornadoes, and hail damage, and because of them we may fear we are forgotten or cursed. Yet we are blessed. Think of the apostle Paul, who suffered thirty-nine lashes from the Jews *five times;* was beaten with rods *three times;* was stoned; shipwrecked *three times;* adrift at sea; in danger from rivers, robbers, cities, the wilderness, sea, betrayal, hunger and thirst, cold and exposure (2 Corinthians 11:24–28). Yet if Paul were to boast, "I will boast of the things that show my weakness" (2 Corinthians 11:30).

There is a temptation to believe that blessings are always accompanied by strength, happiness, courage, or wealth. Really, one can be blessed and struggle. One can be blessed and weak, afraid, or persecuted. One can be blessed during calamities and death.

God can turn to us in favor wherever we are and no matter what we have gone through. He sends His Word as He sent His Son. He forgives sin and cleanses unrighteousness, covering shame and healing wounds.

God does not rely on us: we rely on Him, and the power of Christ does not need our strength, courage, or anything else. In Christ, we are highly favored, which means *blessed,* by our heavenly Father.

Lies

The devil belittles God's gifts. He distracts us and tries to confuse us about what God's gifts are. He puts accusations into our mouths toward others and into our ears against ourselves. All the devil can do is deny, distort, and destroy.

The devil whispers his lies:

- † *If you were blessed, you would have gotten that promotion, that green light, or that weight loss you were looking for.*
- † *If you were blessed, you'd be more successful.*
- † *If you were blessed, the people in your life would be different. Things would be easier. There would be less pain and discomfort.*
- † *If you were blessed, you'd be happy.*
- † *If you were blessed, people would love you, and your children would stay in the church.*
- † *If you were blessed, you would pray enough, do enough, and feel enough to get through this better.*

He alters his tactics here and there. "If you were lucky, your life would be different." "If you were successful, you would finally be accepted." "If only you were *enough* . . ."

The devil claims to have all the kingdoms of the world and their glory (Matthew 4:8), and he dangles them before us, but it is to distract us from God's Word. It is to divert us from trusting God's promise to provide. It is to distort the revelation that our heavenly Father has put all things under Jesus Christ, our Lord (Ephesians 1:19–23).

Blessings are not under Satan's purview, nor are they left to chance or impersonal channels. God is the source of every blessing. That is, every blessing starts with Him. As David wrote, "Oh, how abundant is Your goodness, which You have stored up for those who fear You and worked for those who take refuge in You, in the sight of the children of mankind!" (Psalm 31:19).

The devil whispers, "What of the parents of an unhealthy child?" "People must not be praying hard enough." "Has God really blessed you?" "Did God really say . . . ?" And God answers at length through thirty-nine books of the Old Testament, twenty-seven books of the New Testament, and the persons of Jesus Christ and His Holy Spirit.

The lepers were healed by Christ, not by prayers or by belonging to a certain group of people. They were healed as a sign of God's mercy in Jesus. King David lost his child, his daughter was raped, and his son tried to overthrow his reign as king. He had to beg God for mercy after abusing his power and bringing death where he ought to have offered protection. Still, God had mercy on him and sent us Jesus through his bloodline.

As history indicates, our wants do not define blessings. We can want a lot of very good things, but they may not become ours. All too often what we want can become a stumbling block, distracting us from a life of faith. Or, they could alter something or someone else. Who but our Lord knows what they might affect?

In addition to those very good things we may want, we may want ease more than anything else. So far, however, the request that the valley of the shadow of death also be full of cheer, equal opportunities, and smooth pavement has received a negative answer, much to our personal disappointment.

There are blessed people, but not because God resorts to luck. Neither the term nor the concept of luck is found in the writings of Scripture. There are mysteries that must be revealed before they can be understood, and God works when and where He wishes (John 3:8), but blessings are not given or received according to how we perceive things. Instead, God gives according to His Word.

The devil may imply that blessing floats cliquishly around the most moral and pious of religious people or that it serves as a materialistic line between the *haves* and the *have nots*. Those are against Scripture, as we will see. Nor does Scripture describe blessings as an inner assurance, a mystic experience, or a warm fuzziness.

When our heavenly Father saw the fall into sin, He did not first address our emotions, self-esteem, or other needs humanly perceived. He entered the battle for our souls. He promised His Son, who permanently fulfills God's first blessing toward us: in Christ, the Seed of woman gains dominion of all, releasing us from slavery and reuniting us to the Father.

Although Satan wants to paint a different picture, Jesus remains our perfect blessing. Despite the many and various things we may want or go through, our Savior is the fulfillment of God's promises to us. He is our saving grace. He is our rich inheritance, our assurance, courage, and fortitude. He is our peace beyond understanding.

God's Revelation

"I'm so blessed" may be an expression trotted out at reunions, Thanksgiving, and promotion parties, but blessing is not entirely about you or me. "I'm so blessed" . . . by *whom*? Blessing speaks something about both the blesser and the blessed.

The devil may want to mask that portion of the truth, but the fact remains that blessing is not synonymous with success. While success is about what we may have or what we have accomplished, blessing is about God and His goodwill toward us.

John 15 reads: "Remember the word that I said to you: 'A servant is not greater than his master.' If they persecuted Me, they will also persecute you. If they kept My word, they will also keep yours" (John 15:20). Christian life is a life with crosses, *daily* crosses. Even so, "Blessed are those whose lawless deeds are forgiven, and whose sins are covered" (Romans 4:7).

Blessings are not scores, grades, or popularity contests. Nor are they mysteries we need to discover, only to wander through endless interpretation. Blessings are revealed in Scripture, assuring us of God's promises and reminding us of His favor toward us in Jesus Christ.

The absolute indicator on whether one has been blessed is Jesus. Jesus came to seek and save the lost (Luke 19:10). Are you not lost without Him? Has God's Word come to you? God's Word does not return void (Isaiah 55:11). Have you been baptized (1 Peter 3:21)?

Crosses and blessings are not at odds with each other. By a cross, Christ gained victory for our eternal blessing. In the Old Testament, the faithful sought favor for their sacrifices, and we, too, have sacrifices we make as we take up our cross daily (Luke 9:23).

God has turned His face in favor toward this world in a permanent, indissolvable way. That turning and that gracious face seeking our good is a blessing already fulfilled for every one of us. God's sacrifice has been offered and accepted. The debt of sin has been paid. God's Word goes forth producing faith out of nothing, even as the Creator created the world out of nothing. His Son entered into creation and took manhood forever into Himself.

As we look at what God reveals to be blessings, and our own abilities to bless, there can be a temptation to equate personal successes or easy times with how we are doing. Instead, let us always remember the blessings of the incarnation, cross, and resurrection: redemption, justification, sanctification, and eternal salvation.

God's blessings are a gift. He needs no repayment, though He certainly inspires thanks and praise. He may use them sometimes as an enticement or reward, but they are entirely in the hands of the most benevolent giver (James 1:17; Matthew 7:11; Luke 11:13).

As we proceed through this book and consider a term and concept often bandied about casually, let us guard against misconceptions, misunderstandings, and deceptions. The world is not neutral regarding God's Seed: it is against Him. Our own understanding often falls short, and the devil is quick to have his say. To know the truth, we must turn our eyes and ears to what God's Word teaches.

CHAPTER 2

Language

When I was in college, a girl sneezed, and I automatically responded, "Bless you!" Much to my surprise, she was taken aback. Only later did she explain that she was offended by the overtly religious nature of the expression.

In my mind, I said a good-natured, if somewhat superstitious, thing. She, however, realized before I did that blessings, even in simple, everyday ways, are a religious act. She understood an implied "*God* bless you," and that offended her.

Even though I had spoken as a reflex, I introduced a worldview into our brief interaction. I expressed both a belief in a benefactor and a supposition that He can improve things.

On the positive side of things, I wished good toward her. On the negative, she inferred that I found her, or her situation, lacking in some way or in need. Because of a dwindling cultural impulse toward sharing *gesundheit,* which is German for "good health to you," a sneeze became a quasi-religious moment.

Something as random as a sneeze has now introduced us to a wide spectrum of matters pertaining to blessing:

- † *Words are not always received well!*
- † *Blessings are not always understood.*
- † *Blessings are not always wanted.*
- † *Blessings are not determined by the receiver.*
- † *Blessings are positive or well-intended but call upon One with higher power.*
- † *Blessings imply a relationship between the powerful One and the giver.*

Blessings in a diverse society can be complicated. What does the giver understand himself to be doing? What does the recipient receive? Questions can spiral into philosophical, linguistic, and semantic arenas until one asks, "What does such a word even mean?"

Whether words are religious or not, they are part of language, and language is a good gift of God. It is not the simplest gift to understand, as the tower of Babel illustrates and explains (Genesis 11). Unified and inspiring, man can use language to do almost anything (Genesis 11:6), yet at times it seems more than we can handle.

Linguists and translators have approaches, systems, and philosophies toward understanding and deciphering language, and we are very much blessed by their dedication to their fields. These are fields of science, where careful attention and analysis form hypotheses, arguments, experiments, and conclusions. Thanks be to God that even unbelieving linguists have contributed to the continuity of Scripture and brought the Bible into our hands.

> Linguistics studies language.
> Lexicology studies words.
> Semantics studies word meanings and development.
> "That's just semantics" can mean either
> "We are trying to say the same thing"
> or "You are looking for what isn't there!"

Exegesis

Linguistically related abilities translate Scripture objectively and accurately, bringing God's good news to generation after generation, as well as journeying into the language of every tribe and nation. In a similar vein, theologians practice a discipline known as exegesis. Pronounced ek-sə-jē-səs, it is a scientific, objective analysis of the text. It asks, "What did the author intend to say?" When applied to Scripture, we consider both the human author who wrote the text and the Author of life, who inspired and continues to work through the text.

However, despite human attempts toward unbiased science, not everyone values exegesis as a practice. It is becoming increasingly popular to suggest that it is the responsibility of the reader to add meaning to the text.

You have probably seen questions such as "How do you interpret the text?" or "What does that mean to you?" The questions can be relatively harmless. At the same time, they can also begin to elevate human understanding over the written Word of God.

People can be so confident of their own discernment that, knowingly or unknowingly, they place their own thoughts or feelings above the Bible itself. Some church bodies write such practices into their beliefs, often under their understanding of Scripture. Subjectivity becomes a basis for their entire religious system with an understandable effect upon church teaching, receiving and giving pastoral care, mission work, fellowship, and morality.

The technical term is eisegesis (pronounced ī-sə-jē-səs). While exegesis is a scientific, objective analysis of text, eisegesis promotes a subjective, personal interpretation. It intentionally introduces one's own assumptions, desires, emotions, and fears into the text.

> Exegesis "reads out" while eisegesis "reads into" text. Biblical exegesis relates to translation from the original languages of Scripture:
>
> - Hebrew (Hebrew gets its name from Eber, a descendant of Shem mentioned in Genesis 10:21–24)
> - Aramaic (another Semitic language that dominated the Fertile Crescent for more than a thousand years, starting in the 500s BC and giving way to the prominence of Arabic in the AD 700s)
> - Greek
>
> Exegetical tools typically include the following:
>
> - Language study (including grammar and poetic forms)
> - Word studies
> - Dictionaries, concordances (track word usage within a work), and lexicons (index how the term is used in other places, including scrolls, papyri, engravings, codices, books)
> - Hermeneutics (principles of interpretation)

Eisegesis is an attempt to personalize biblical texts.

- Focus may be on an ideas or emotion with Scripture in a secondary, supporting role.
- Passages may be isolated from larger context, intentionally or unintentionally, in order to be used as a proof-text.

This is not to say that questions about "you" are necessarily inappropriate. The distinction is to clarify the teachings of God. How you react to a text may be relevant to those sharing your burdens, as God instructs in Galatians 6:2; however, that is entirely separate from what God reveals through His eternal Word.

For example, a teenager could interpret the commandment "You shall not commit adultery" in a very narrow sense. The Church, however, has an intricate understanding of sin and temptation, marriage and the body, creation and vocation, and how marriage relates to Christ and His faithfulness to us as the divine Bridegroom. A simple word search for "adultery" may not unlock all those thematic connections, but careful reading of Scripture and the study of language can.

Questions about a person are often necessary to serve them in a personalized way through our vocations. By asking how the modern teen understands marriage and adultery, one can learn what additional discussions one may need to have that he or she may grow in God's Word. But without building upon Scripture—the foundation of the apostles and prophets, Christ Jesus Himself being the cornerstone (Ephesians 2:20–21)—the individual can be deceived into thinking his or her thoughts easily reflect God's thoughts.

So, while it may seem silly to suggest a person could confuse his or her own perspective with the revelation of God, this is all around us. We can think of the Book of Judges. Even the Israelites, who were so close in time to God's miraculous deeds, did what was evil in the sight of the Lord, turning from God to pursue their own pleasures.

Church bodies are not shy about stating their positions on the authority of Scripture. Look on their official websites. How does the congregation or denomination describe individuals or learning from God? Is the Bible described as the Word of God or *containing* the Word of God? Is the Bible beloved but not described as authoritative or powerful?

Context

Context matters. I said, "Bless you," and while I thought it was a generally safe expression, it made the woman angry. She very much felt I had imposed my religious beliefs upon her.

The context at large now is a society in which gay marriage and Planned Parenthood are blessed freely, but blessing a sneeze can be too religious to welcome. Even beyond mincing or misusing religious terminology, non-Christians loudly denounce, "That isn't Christian!" without ever having read Scripture or attended a Christian church service. Words are so stripped of their context that "God is love" becomes an ungodly excuse to do whatever feels pleasurable.

It is no wonder, then, that people can have such diverse reactions to Christian terminology. Christians themselves may disagree on meaning, application, and significance of nearly anything. And if the sacred Scriptures ultimately boil down to "How I personally see things," unbelievers have even less reason to listen to the Bible passages people are so prone to throw their way.

Society joins Pontius Pilate in asking, "What is truth?" (John 18:38). All sorts of words are abused, particularly words in the Bible, as sinners wrestle with God's revelations on sin and salvation. Many simply want words to mean something else (i.e., marriage, love, fetus, sin, grace).

But ours is a God who binds Himself to us through His Word, both spoken and incarnate. He is the great I AM (Exodus 3:14). He is the definition of love (1 John 4:8). He is the Author of life (Acts 3:15). The triune God sends, embodies, and testifies concerning His Word, which creates and sustains.

By His own working, believers do not need to add anything to Scripture: God has already granted meaning to the text. The Holy Spirit gives the Bible its value despite—rather than through—the many imagined interpretations of Holy Scripture.

Studying the breadth of Scripture is literally foundational for the members of the household of God (Ephesians 2:19–22). We are to hear and read the words—words that can be parsed and put into context. We are to cling to the Word God has given us (Psalm 119:31) and give thanks for such an infinite gift. This is not because our grasp is so strong or our understanding so penetrating, but because *with text* God weaves us into Himself, teaching us while also breathing new life into us and equipping us with His gifts.

Analysis

Considering blessing in an analytical way reveals a sub-layer of promise stretching throughout Scripture. Seeking an objective, respectful approach to Scripture, we incorporate elements of academic study into translation and theological work.

People have all too quickly presumed that theology is opposed to science. Rather, the revelation of God is uniquely capable of supporting close examination. Pastors and theologians in our Lutheran tradition routinely have religious texts in their original languages with lexicons that help in translation. Laity at home may have, in addition to regular dictionaries, Bible dictionaries, concordances, and Christian encyclopedias.[1] To resurrect a beautiful expression from the Middle Ages, we can recognize theology to be Queen of the Sciences.

Our God reveals Himself and His will through His words, which build upon themselves. He does not mince words. If He recorded something in Scripture, once or a hundred times, it is His Word. He has caused the expression to stand for thousands of years.

As those who have received Scripture from our gracious God, we can read a passage closely and consider it in the context of other passages. For example, the narrow context of Gabriel's announcement to Mary shows us she would bear a child (Luke 1:26–38), while the broader teaching of Scripture shows us the impact on us all. Some texts have more narrow recipients than others, but increasingly wide context includes that God has given each passage of the Bible as a revelation to the Church and all Christians for His own purpose—and that includes preaching to crowds, masses, and anyone who has ears. *All* that has been taught by Christ is to be brought to all nations (Matthew 28:19–20).

Sometimes something as simple as seeing who "powers" the verb is enough to remind us that much Scripture is about what God does for sinners, rather than what sinners need to do for God. Immediate context helps us understand the Bible.

Context plays the major role in determining meaning, even for individual words. Linguists have discovered that information in a spoken or written communication is repeated to a large extent to avoid misinterpretations. Which is to say, even a narrow parameter of context can be telling. Broader examination, with additional passages and changing scenarios, allows definitive meanings to be accepted.

Our study of the Hebrew term *brk* benefits from such linguistic approaches. There are a large number of occurrences, both within Scripture and from other places, providing a clear picture of the word's meaning, even with shades of nuances and contextual anomalies. When we consider *brk* in the Old Testament, we can look at how it is used in other similar situations to help clarify exactly what is being said.

For our purposes, context specifically shows us how the blessing is accomplished, what its purpose is, and who blesses whom. Is God blessing man, man blessing man, or man blessing God?

Still, *our* context would happily jumble up eisegesis with exegesis. To clarify that, there is a hermeneutical principle—a guideline related to interpreting text—that states, "Scripture interprets Scripture."

Scripture interprets Scripture, and suddenly it becomes clear that blessings are intertwined with creation, the incarnation, Israel, redemption, the paradise to come, and more. Within the thematic use of blessing within Scripture, we can see our human needs addressed by a God who turns graciously toward us with favor. We can see an encouragement to pray and call upon God in all circumstances. We can see the ultimate lengths that God took to restore us to a relationship with Him through His Son.

BRK

The common feature of all the meanings of *brk* is that blessing, whether it consists of a speech act (benediction) or a physical act (benefaction), is an act freely performed that expresses the grace and goodwill of the blesser. It has the connotation of a favorable relationship between the blesser and the person blessed.

Benediction = to speak good to
Benefaction = to do good to

That means, among other things, that we cannot coerce God into granting us blessing. We might think of Jacob, who wrestled with God. He did get blessed that night, but not because of his strength. Instead, when he was weakened, he received a new name and was blessed—they did not part as enemies, but on positive terms. In Jacob, God kept His promises to Abraham and Isaac, and to all of us, to send a Savior, the Seed of woman. Jacob clung to God, sought His name, and limped his passage of faith, as so many of us do.

As we will see from Scripture, God's blessing is not only an expression between God and one man, but it is also a visible sign of His favor before others. It attracts the attention of others and makes them desire God's blessing too. Consider the nation of Israel: Because of God's blessing, "Everyone who sees them [Israel] will recognize that they are the people whom Yahweh has blessed" (Isaiah 61:9 CM); "all nations will consider you [Israel] blessed because you are a desirable land" (Malachi 3:12 CM; cf. v. 10). With regard to individuals, others say, "We have seen quite clearly that Yahweh is with you" (CM) because God had blessed them (Genesis 26:28; see also Genesis 39:2–6).

God's blessing can be as grand as a prosperous, unconquered kingdom, and as intimate as a wedding night or hiccups in the womb. They can be corporate, to a nation or to believers, or personal, to Hannah or the Virgin Mary. They can even be a step removed, like when God calls Egypt and Assyria, as well as Israel, *baruk* in Isaiah 19:25; the context makes clear that "blessed" means that the two countries will have a covenantal relationship with God just as Israel does. That is, God blesses the countries according to His covenant with Israel, and so they are recipients of blessing.

Thematic Use

Blessings are pervasive throughout Scripture, implicitly and explicitly. God wants to be known as He who blesses, and He wants

His relationships characterized by a blesser/blessed relationship. He gives, and we receive. He prepares, and we benefit. He speaks, and we flourish.

Although He blesses in a great variety of ways, and to a wide spectrum of receivers, they come together in a revealing picture of His love and grace. He generously sows His blessing. He gives without seeking payment, and He sends His Son despite His servants being mistreated and abused.

His favor is well worth seeking. It is far reaching and life giving. Noah found favor in the eyes of the Lord, and mankind survived the flood (Genesis 6:8). Abraham found favor, and so the Lord did not pass him by, but promised him a child through whom all nations would be blessed (Genesis 18:3; 12:3). The greatest feat, however, is the fulfillment of that promise, as Christ joins us to Himself (Romans 6:4–5; 1 Corinthians 6:17). So that, whenever God turns His face in favor to the Son, He also turns His face in favor to us.

Every blessing that the Father would give the Son, the Son shares with those joined to Him. Not because we earned it with our works, and not because we sought it with such strength. Rather, it is because God approached us with His Word. He sent His Spirit to hover over the waters. He sent His Son to die in order that those who have died with Christ will also live with Him (Romans 6:3–11).

Our God speaks His words of blessing and makes them be so. He takes it upon Himself to create, provide, sustain, save, justify, and sanctify. "All this He does out of fatherly, divine goodness and mercy, without any merit or worthiness in me. For all this it is my duty to thank and praise, serve and obey Him. This is most certainly true."[2]

The theme of blessing is an integral, powerful element throughout the Bible. God's blessings of man and the animals in the primeval history are indicative of His favorable attitude toward the creation. The major concern of the patriarchal narratives is to trace the transmission and fulfillment of God's blessing promise through the succeeding generations. The attainment of blessing is the motivating factor for observing the Sinai covenant. The Wisdom Literature also says that man's reward for Torah piety is blessing. In their apocalyptic visions, the prophets foresee a time when God's deliverance will usher in a golden age of blessing. So many blessings! And they reveal much about our almighty, loving God!

Human blessings likewise play a central role in the Bible. People uttered blessings on many occasions. The patriarchs delivered their deathbed testaments in the form of blessings. The Priestly Blessing was a central element of temple worship. Prayers were often uttered in the form of blessings. Blessings were spoken in everyday life situations such as greetings and departing, marriages, thanking others, and expressing friendship. So many blessings reveal how people, too, can love and serve within creation.

People often expressed praise toward God by means of blessing formulas and other forms of *brk*, both in secular settings and in the religious ritual. At times, God was praised for specific actions, while at other times He was praised because of His character and qualities—which corresponds in a way with human blessings, as sometimes man blesses man because of specifics or because of more general character or qualities. The Psalms in particular encourage the joyful praise of God and assert that it is man's duty to do so.

As context broadens our understanding, we will consider each blessing and be catechized anew. We will hear with the ears of faith that God gives His blessings, yes, even to—and through—our own struggling flesh and blood. And every single blessing traces back to that perfect Man who gives His flesh and blood for our eternal—and daily—salvation.

One cannot always anticipate reactions to religious words, and religious words are everywhere. Avoiding them altogether is nearly impossible, as we will see. Underlining that is the basic truth that words of Scripture *are* words of daily life. They are not a different, inaccessible language, but a gift given to our ears, mouths, and eyes, as we receive God's revelation. Religious language remains a basic form of communication, within religious circles or outside of them.

What a tremendous blessing that the triune God reveals Himself a word at a time, and also through paragraphs, pages, books, and two testaments! And, in addition to the effective work of the Holy Spirit through those words, the Father sends His Son as the Word Incarnate. When we fail to stand, there is still Jesus. When we fail to grasp, there is still Christ. And blessing, as you will see, is the multifaceted groundwork beneath the surface of much of God's revelation.

CHAPTER 3

Creation Blessings

We may think God blesses creation only in an abstract sense, but does He? In the beginning, what did God bless? He made the waters swarm with living creatures and the expanse of the heavens with every winged bird (Genesis 1:20–21). God saw that it was good, and then He blessed them, saying, "Be fruitful and multiply and fill the waters in the seas, and let birds multiply on the earth" (Genesis 1:22).

Before there was any action apart from day, night, and sprouting, God blessed. He made living creatures and turned His favor toward them.

And, having revealed to us that He blessed at that point, He teaches us something good to remember. Blessings are sometimes rewards, but they are never payments—only gifts God gives as He chooses.

His favor is not reserved for spiritual exercises or feats of strength. Instead, the Creator of heaven and earth plants a garden and provides food for "every living thing" (Job 12:10; Psalm 145:16). The almighty God makes us clothing and covers our shame. He considers even ravens and lilies of the field (Luke 12:24–28).

Rather than scorn mundane life with its humble, repetitive needs, our Creator elevates what so often we take for granted. While we dismiss and grumble about creation, He continues to work through it.

For our sake, the Creator works through creation to show us His love and favor. He gives to us in ways He made us able to receive. For our sake, He gives mouths and sound waves to carry the very Word of God, and ears and eyes to take possession of it. He grants blessing through such common elements as water, bread, and wine, for daily and heavenly bread. And, for our sake, the Word that is God took creation into Himself, the Son of God becoming God and man.

Fertility

We may live in a time that is so fearful of fertility—fecundophobia—and so generally self-distancing from it that stores sell infertile fruit, but from the Genesis creation narrative, it is easy to see why blessing is closely associated with fertility. Fertility is such a commonly given blessing that it is sometimes considered an original meaning of blessing! This book will discuss many more things than simply fertility, but extolling fertility can rightly be understood as praising the ongoing blessing of God within creation.

What exactly is happening in Genesis 1 when God blesses? Is He blessing fertility, or is He blessing *with* fertility? Put another way, is God changing the creation He had just pronounced good (Genesis 1:21–22)?

In parallel passages in Genesis 1:22, 28; 9:1–7; 35:9–12, there is no indication that the blessing bestowed fertility upon Noah or Jacob. Rather, God encourages Adam and Eve, and others, to reproduce. God is revealing His favor toward man and procreation. Presumably, part of that was because the population was so small (as the text specifies "fill the earth" with Adam, Eve, and Noah), but that is not explicitly stated regarding Jacob. Perhaps in Jacob we can see God's ultimate concern to fill to full capacity the wedding feast of His Son.

These later examples make clear that, while fertility is certainly a form of blessing in itself, God is making an announcement. He pronounces a benediction—a statement "to speak well of" or "to bless"—and the speaking itself is the act of blessing.

That in no way belittles the blessing or the power of God's Word. "Be fruitful and multiply and fill the earth" (Genesis 1:28) "is ever effective in nature, so that [the earth] is fruitful and multiplies" by its power, as we continue to confess.[1] Still, the fact that the indicative form of the verb *berak* was chosen rather than a verb of command or order illustrates a point.

God's blessing of the birds and sea creatures in Genesis 1:22 is equivalent to God saying, "I hereby declare My desire for you to reproduce and so fill the earth" (CM). This blessing becomes a formula, drawn upon as a recurring theme and descriptor that invokes the larger realities of God and His world.

The swarms of living creatures in the sea and the birds across the expanse of the heavens are to be fruitful, multiply, and fill the sea and earth. Man, also, is to increase, with the additional task of dominion. It is ingrained within all creation. Martin Luther has a wonderful sermon on the human compulsion to be in a family through the powerful echoes of God's words "Be fruitful and multiply."[2] By God pronouncing His blessing, He also reveals His goodwill and favor toward it all.

Also in the Genesis 1 passage, there are imperatives God uses to follow the blessing as He addresses man: "subdue the earth and rule over the fish . . ." (1:28 CM). By them, God explains the natural order already built by God into creation (also in vv. 29–30).

There is a distinction between pronouncing a blessing and other forms of blessing. At times, the simple revelation of God's goodwill is a sufficient blessing: things are not altered further. Still, it is significant that God graciously reveals His approval, and that approval is ongoing and steadfast.

Even now, while we lack the ability to exercise perfect dominion over the earth because of sin, it remains God's desire—a desire fulfilled in Jesus' perfect dominion over heaven and earth and all things (Colossians 1:16)—for the meek to inherit the earth (Matthew 5:5). Though not all are able to have children, Jesus stretches out His hand and says, "Here are My mother and My brothers!" (Matthew 12:49).

And He Still Provides

Fertility and dominion become ongoing themes. Fertility certainly includes children, but it also gains direct connotations of prosperity. Bearing much fruit makes for a bountiful harvest. Fertile animals create an abundance and grow wealth in the forms of plentiful food, clothes, and trade. Fertility and prosperity are commonly associated with a bright future and a lasting legacy.

The Lord, who made heaven and earth, shows through creation that He is a God of blessing by bestowing life, fertility, and His favor upon creation (Genesis 1:22, 28; 2:3; 5:2; cf. Genesis 14:19; Psalm

124:8). This is a theological understanding beneath the historical phrasing "who made heaven and earth" (Psalm 115:15). The Lord blesses creation and turns favorably to it. This positive attention is what gains the psalmist's trust, in addition to the efficacy of God's Word. Because of our Lord's steadfastness, His blessing is assuredly ongoing, building off of the historical significance that He created and maintains all things.

Genesis 1:22, 28; 5:2 are evidence regarding God's attitude toward creation in its entirety. God's blessing is not used only to fulfill a promise or even to help His own people. He also blesses to maintain creation, which benefits all mankind.

God has made His blessing a regular part of created order. It is not limited to certain times and places. Rather, the Piel of *brk* comes to means "to bestow those things necessary for abundant plant and animal life," such as rain, dew, fertile soil, and so on.

> Pronounced *pē-yel,* Piel is one of seven major verb stems.
> It indicates intensive action and active voice.
> (Pual is similar to Piel, except that Pual is passive
> —the subject receives the action of the verb.)
> *Brk* means to bless and to bless intensely, or to make thrive.

So while fertility is one potentially defining point of blessing, sustaining life is another. God favors life. The Father gives life (John 5:21), the Son is the Author of life (Acts 3:15), and the Holy Spirit is the Lord and Giver of life (Job 33:4; Genesis 2:7).

Such sustaining is best understood to mean *thrive.* God certainly makes us thrive through the power of His Word. He also makes us thrive through creation and its natural processes. He works through sun and rain. He works through our ability to marry and procreate. He works through mouths, ears, and eyes that we may receive—and be blessed by—His Word.

Consider these verses. In Genesis, Isaac said, "The smell of my son is as the smell of a field that the LORD has blessed!" (Genesis 27:27), and the Lord says in Isaiah:

Thus says the LORD:

"As the new wine is found in the cluster,
    and they say, 'Do not destroy it,
    for there is a blessing in it,'
so I will do for My servants' sake,
and not destroy them all." (Isaiah 65:8)

While we may be familiar with the idea of God considering ravens and lilies (Luke 12:24–28), He considers a cluster of grapes too. And by them He remembers His own handiwork forming creation and man. By them He respects the blessings He has previously given, and "so I will do for My servants' sake, and not destroy them all" (Isaiah 65:8).

There are thorns, thistles, and sweat in this life (Genesis 3:18–19). There are tribulations and persecutions, cares of the world, deceit, and desires for other things (Mark 4:14–20). Yet consider Psalm 65:9–13, which describes how God provides plants and animals through the natural processes. Dr. Mitchell translates verse 10 to read, "You drench the earth's furrows, level its ridges; You soften it with abundant showers, You bless its plants."

The triune God gives us our daily bread and much more besides. He maintains creation for all people and does so in part through how He established the world. Not only that life would go on, but that creation would thrive through His gifts.

Other Blessings in the Creation Narratives

Our Lord does not hesitate to bless simple things. He blesses by speaking actual words. He uses water for "the washing of regeneration and renewal of the Holy Spirit, whom He poured out on us richly through Jesus Christ our Savior" (Titus 3:5–6). He uses bread and wine. And when He blesses, He gives something great indeed: His goodwill.

When God blessed man in Genesis 1:28, He did more than bless babies. He did more than grant dominion. After making man in His own image, He looked kindly to mankind. He created and maintained a personal relationship, as seen in walking among them frequently enough that they could recognize the sound (Genesis 3:8).

In His favorable grace, our Lord used His Word to interact: to teach, prohibit, warn, inquire, and answer. And even when His Word was no longer trusted—for a fruit delightful to the eye and promising wisdom (Genesis 3:6)—the Lord God did not curse His blessed Adam. Instead, the ground bears His curse, though certainly created good and bountiful (Genesis 3:17; 1:10–13).

There is a profound and extensive faithfulness with which God keeps His blessings. It becomes a layer within the context of His actions toward all humanity. How does He save man? By blessed fertility—woman's Seed (Genesis 3:15), the Child who receives dominion over heaven and earth, the Second Adam (1 Corinthians 15:45), and a firstfruit (1 Corinthians 15:20–23).

God's blessing reveals His relationship and commitment to us as His goodwill and favor come upon us through His Word and gifts. Notice that they come in ways we can naturally receive, and His Word retains a central position.

In three verses, God's oral blessing denotes consecration (Genesis 2:3; Exodus 20:11; 32:29.[3]) The meaning "consecrate" is a meaning specialized from the more general meaning "pronounce a blessing formula." In consecration, God issues a declaration that changes the status of a person or thing.

> Piel and Pual verbs can be difficult to understand or translate, even for a scholar. Here is a selection of meanings for Piel *brk:*
>
> - To pronounce God's blessing
> - To bestow those things necessary for abundant life
> - To make thrive
> - To consecrate (change status)
> - To greet with a benediction or to farewell
> - To treat with respect or treat well
> - To recognize or seek blessing
> - To praise God

At the close of the creation narrative, God blesses the seventh day: "God blessed the seventh day and sanctified it because on it He rested from all His work which He had done in creating" (Genesis 2:3 CM). His blessing consecrates the seventh day as a holy day. The blessing and naming does not change the object—the day remains a day—but the blessing changes the status. It adds a layer of significance, in this account particularly in the sight of God.

Here "holy" means only that the day commemorates God's activity. God remembers the Sabbath and that all of creation is His handiwork. Perhaps this is similar to the rainbow, which God remembers as a sign of His covenant with "every living creation of all flesh that is on the earth" (Genesis 9:16–17).

Exodus 20:8–11, on the other hand, discusses the implications of the consecration of the day for man. God consecrated the day and told mankind so they would remember His gracious provision and the words that revealed it to them. Because man has an opportunity to rest and be refreshed, God made the Sabbath an additional source of blessing for man.

Let us refer to Luther's Small Catechism to consider this point. The Sabbath Day is made holy by God's Word. Adam and Eve did not witness creation, and Adam was asleep when God crafted Eve. The first parents learned about creation in the same way we do: God's Word. And God spoke His Word that they might trust Him.

Moses also describes a Sabbath year—every seventh year, the Israelites were to leave all their fields fallow—and an oddity occurs in Leviticus 25:20–22.

> And if you say, "What shall we eat in the seventh year, if we may not sow or gather in our crop?" I will command My blessing on you in the sixth year, so that it will produce a crop sufficient for three years. When you sow in the eighth year, you will be eating some of the old crop; you shall eat the old until the ninth year, when its crop arrives.

The blessing is actually pictured as an independent entity to be sent by God. This unusual image, thankfully, has something of a parallel in Deuteronomy 28:8. There, however, it is clear that God commanding the blessing is still God Himself blessing. The implication, then, is that Leviticus 25 is likewise figurative language. Psalm 133:3 has the same expression, qualifying *berakah* as "life." God promises to give life by His Word.

Here is an extension of the initial Sabbath blessing. Because creation is God's work and not our own, creation does not depend on us. Rather, we along with all creation are under the ultimate care of God. God blessed the Sabbath, and through the power of His blessing both God and the day continue to bless us.

Naming

There is one more blessing to acknowledge in creation narratives, and that is found in Genesis 5:2. While this could be simply a shortened version of the first two creation accounts, this passage explicitly ties God's blessing with naming.

Genesis 5:2 looks back on 1:28 and states that God named man in conjunction with blessing him: "He blessed them and named them *'adam* at the time that they were created" (CM). The Piel of *brk* here means to pronounce the blessing formula in 1:28. The actual naming probably occurred in 1:26. Naming was an essential part of creation, since each creature, including man, must have a label to identify its place in the created order.

A name from God marks the entrance into a relationship with God. In Genesis 2:19–20, Adam entered a relationship with animals while naming them and discovered no helper fit for him. God said He would make a helper fit for Adam, and He fulfilled that promise. Then, as God brought Eve to Adam in marriage, Adam named her.

Receiving a new name is a blessing with tangible benefits to help assure the recipients of God's ongoing blessing. In Adam's case, the name also signified man's place within the natural order, functioning as God's representative on earth because he was made in God's image.

In the patriarchal narratives, God several times blesses by bestowing new names in conjunction with issuing the blessing promises (Genesis 17:5, 15; cf. 32:27–29). The significance of the renaming is that it denotes conferral of a new status. It marks the entrance of the patriarchs into a relationship with God in which they will be the recipients of the promised blessing.

The act of renaming is more important than the meaning of the new names. While the blessings were still only promises, the new names were tangible benefits that the patriarchs received immediately to help assure them of God's future blessing. The names were an extension of His promise.

We, too, receive new names as new creations of God. We become little christs—anointed ones—by Baptism. Scripture even speaks in terms of God's name being placed upon us. We are also under the names of our spiritual fathers, Abraham and Israel. In Isaiah 44:5, we see the repentant "name himself by the name of Israel." We are also right to think of Romans 4:16: he who shares the faith of Abraham has Abraham as his father. The repentant and faithful want to share in the names and statuses God has given.

In our case, we receive the name of the Father and of the Son and of the Holy Spirit upon our forehead and heart in Baptism. And, as we assemble in the name of the Lord Jesus (1 Corinthians 5:4), our status is that of child of God, incorporated into the only-begotten Son.

A Few More Comments on Fertility

A woman exclaimed with a loud cry, "Blessed is the womb that bore You, and the breasts at which You nursed!" (Luke 11:27). Here was a woman who delighted in the abilities God had given her female body. Here is an example of elevating motherhood and honoring procreation! And she was right. Mary is blessed. She is the "favored one" (Luke 1:28). But Jesus does not leave the mother pondering her own desire, which could have been to have Jesus as her own. Instead, He says, "Even more blessed are those who hear the Word of God and keep it" (Luke 11:28, alt. translation).

Mary, the mother of our Lord, was doubly blessed as she was both Jesus' mother and His follower. Yet, each one of us is equally blessed with her. There is no higher blessing than hearing God's Word and recognizing by the power of the Holy Spirit the treasure that it is.

I had a friend comment to me that American evangelicals hear

"Be fruitful and multiply" and interpret it to mean "Knock on doors! Grow the church!" Lutherans hear the same and say, "Babies!"

There are various interpretations and extrapolations from the Genesis 1:26–30 texts, which we need not address here. It is clear, however, that fertility should be honored and blessed by us, insofar as we are able. At the same time, fertility is not an essential element of blessing. It is the relationship between giver and receiver, between God and the person blessed, that makes a blessing a blessing. God turns in favor to all who are in Christ, and God certainly causes fruitfulness in areas outside of parenthood (Galatians 5:22–23).

Reproductive fertility lasts only a certain personalized length of time for men and women (excluding Abraham, Sarah, and other miraculous occurrences, of course). Even within that fertile stretch of life, there are regular and recurring periods of infertility, which play a role in life after the fall. Biblical genealogies certainly reveal later birthrates than one might expect. Still, fertility illustrates a few practical things for us:

- † *Blessings can have seasons, ebbs and flows.*
- † *Blessings come according to God's timetable and not our own.*
- † *Blessings can come with great labor.*
- † *By faith, we can pray, watch, and wait, but only God deigns whether certain blessings come.*
- † *Even after receiving a blessing, there can be much uncertainty.*

Ultimately, thanks be to God, God's blessing of fertility points us to His own Son, Jesus, who took our flesh upon Himself. He is the one Child promised to us all, from the first mother and father to the last daughter and son:

> For to us a child is born,
> to us a son is given;
> and the government shall be upon His shoulder,
> and His name shall be called
> Wonderful Counselor, Mighty God,
> Everlasting Father, Prince of Peace. (Isaiah 9:6)

CHAPTER 4

Abraham

Three of the largest world religions claim Abraham as their father: Judaism, Christianity, and Islam. To say he is famous is an understatement. The expression "in the bosom of Abraham"—or less poetically "at his side"—means in the promised land of heaven (Luke 13:28; 16:22–23). He has speaking roles in both the Old and New Testaments, and his name belongs in the litany of "the God of Abraham, Isaac, and Jacob," and his blessing is the reason why.

Abram wasn't born famous. The first mentions of him in Scripture are modest. Like many before him, he was a few bylines in a genealogy. Known primarily for his father, he was mentioned with his wife—and her barrenness—and for moving with his father, Terah, and his nephew Lot.

Although the genealogy of Shem's descendants in Genesis 11:10–26 shows most men after the flood having children in their thirties, Terah was seventy when he fathered Abram, Nahor, and Haran. We can note that Genesis 5 suggests sixty-five was not a young age to begin having children, but Terah is also unusual within the Genesis 11 genealogy as his is the first entry to lack "other sons and daughters." Although Terah, his father, and his son lived well past 145 years, the life-span, as well as the birthrate, appears to be plummeting.

With Sarai, we see a rare mention of a wife within a genealogy, which is to say Sarai would be one woman people were sure to remember. We also see the first mention of infertility within Scripture.

In the broader setting, the world was repopulating after the flood (Genesis 6–9), and God had confused the language of the earth to disperse people over the face of all the earth (Genesis 11:1–9). People had tried to build a tower "with its top in the heavens" (v. 4) and to make a name and legacy for themselves, only to be brought down to their original task of subduing the earth, remembered by name only.

While the builders hoped to seize what they wanted with their own hands, Sarai was a woman unable to do the one task associated solely with her female body: her womb would not bear fruit. No matter what she did, she was not in a position to gift herself, or her husband, with a child. Such inability stands in direct opposition to man's grasping for power and control by any means available.

Sarai's infertility testifies that only God can ultimately provide. Only He bears power and control. It is God who works through His blessing for the good of creation and explicitly includes barren women in the bloodline of the woman's greatest Seed.

Sarai's condition demonstrates that God would go to unusual lengths in order to bless her family and all the world with a child. Sarai was given that promised child, and from the fruit of her barren womb the world also received the promised Child of God. Sarah was barren, and the mother of our Lord was a virgin, yet God would bless the world through woman's seed.

Originally from Ur of the Chaldeans, Terah and Abram planned to move to Canaan, but settled in Haran instead (Genesis 11:27–31). It is ironic to note that when the Lord called Abram to leave, it in one way fulfilled his father Terah's original wish. However, the Lord said:

> Go from your country and your kindred and your father's house to the land that I will show you. And I will make of you a great nation, and I will bless you and make your name great, so that you will be a blessing. I will bless those who bless you, and him who dishonors you I will curse, and in you all the families of the earth shall be blessed. (Genesis 12:1–3)

Abram left his father and his father's house. Lot came with him.

On first reading, this could appear to be a simple prophetic blessing. One might be tempted to say, "How nice for him," and leave it at that, but a pleasant life with grandchildren and good fortune to share is far from the full extent of this blessing. This blessing continues to affect us all, even to this day and forevermore.

Purposes

The text of this blessing includes an introduction from God Himself. Who is God? He is the God without earthly boundary. He is the builder of nations, the one over all lands. He is the one who makes great. He is the blesser who will work through Abram's family to spread His divine blessing throughout the world.

Starting at the beginning of Genesis, we also see Him to be a consistent, steadfast God. How is He blessing? He uses His words. He positions Himself as the provider who makes thrive. He sends man to be a source of blessing. He works through fertility and family growth. He encourages man to spread over all the earth ("fill the earth," Genesis 9:1).

God promised to bless Abram as an expression of His goodwill toward him. Blessing here is not a reward for Abram's prior conduct, as no prior conduct other than marriage and a move are mentioned. God simply approached a man with blessing.

The immediate purpose, then, was to draw Abram into a covenant with Himself. The ultimate purpose corresponds with His previous blessings upon family—that is, properly ordered human fertility (sex within marriage), dominion over the earth, and God's own provision exemplified now in (a) creation, (b) the Sabbath, and (c) the promise of woman's Seed. Functionally, the Abrahamic, or Patriarchal, Blessing ties fatherhood to the woman's Seed.

Of course, we can skip ahead to think of Abram's descendant who ultimately fulfilled this promise and the roles of both Sarai and Abram. It was Jesus, who left His Father at the direction of God. From Jesus, God builds a great kingdom—and the family of the Church—and by Jesus God expands His goodwill and favor toward countless others throughout the world. The Word Himself gives life, makes thrive, and is the epitome of all blessing. Jesus will be blessed, and those who curse Jesus will be cursed! He is the ultimate fulfillment of the promise, giving salvation and eternal life in the name of the triune God!

Still, we should not overlook that the promise was originally given to Abram. Abram received that gift of mediation, although the keys to heaven and hell are not his. God looked upon Abram with favor and bound Himself to a son of earth through a promise.

The focus on Abram, and by extension his family, should not narrow our focus to only the people who would become Israel. God clearly has in mind blessing "all the families of the earth" (Genesis 12:3). God called Abram to be a recipient and also a source of blessing. Still, it should give us pause that God granted such a blessing to a mere mortal, a byline in those genealogies we can be so quick to skim over.

The relative obscurity of Abram before the blessing should highlight for us the exalted position after the blessing. We, too, are one of many within a long stretch of parents and children. We, too, begin in darkened obscurity. We, too, however, are included in the blessing, directly blessed by the Almighty, all-knowing God. We are brought to light and blessing through the Lord's gracious, undeserved favor and by His Holy Word.

God's blessing does not position Abram as a tyrant, distributing blessing as he will. Rather, "he will be a blessing."[1] God calls Abram to be a source of God's own blessing (*berakah,* 12:2), and that blessing is exceedingly generous. The placement of the expression functions as a bridge between the descriptions of Abram's personal blessings in verses 1–2 and the description of how all nations will acquire blessing in verse 3.

It is descriptive indeed to consider the parallel between blessing as goodwill and favor and God promising to bless those who are on good terms with Abram. The friend of a friend appears to be fortunate indeed!

A significant portion of the purpose of this blessing is to bless others through mediation.[2] Though such a status is not as familiar with many of us in these days, God Himself takes it very seriously.

Genesis 18 shows how Abram (renamed Abraham in Genesis 17) was an influential mediator. In Genesis 18:18, the Lord asks, "How can I conceal from Abraham what I am about to do when Abraham will certainly become a great people, and all peoples will acquire blessing through him?" (CM). God reveals his intentions about Sodom's destruction to Abraham because of Abraham's status. Genesis 18:23–33 describes Abraham's intercession for Sodom. Through his efforts, his relatives are spared. One can consider Jesus in a similar predicament.

Part of mediation means that God's blessing is not entirely free-for-all: there are conditions. The conditions are simply not what we might typically expect. God promises to bestow benefits only to those on good terms with Abraham. That is, the Lord is associating Himself with Abraham so closely that those who are hostile to him are also effectively, and cursedly, hostile to God. Still, the final phrasing in 12:3 illustrates a vast amount of people blessed rather than the alternative.

Mediation in no way diminishes the active participation of God. Instead, it draws in additional participants. Our own blessing is mediated by Jesus (1 Timothy 2:5; Hebrews 8:6; 9:15; 12:24). The conditions are not God's Law—although we certainly should strive to obey Him and serve our neighbors with good works—but the Spirit of life:

> For the law of the Spirit of life has set you free in Christ Jesus from the law of sin and death. For God has done what the law, weakened by the flesh, could not do. By sending His own Son in the likeness of sinful flesh and for sin, He condemned sin in the flesh, in order that the righteous requirement of the law might be fulfilled in us, who walk not according to the flesh but according to the Spirit. (Romans 8:2–4)

In addition to the Office of the Holy Ministry as instituted by Jesus, there are other, more secular ways that individuals mediate—or act as intermediaries—in God's blessing. After all, God blesses marriage, and marriage exists between a husband and a wife. God blesses fertility, which again takes two. For all the sweeping blessings on plants and animals, it takes men and women to take care of them and turn them into the necessary daily bread.

There is no chance of confusing the construction of the complementing narrative in Genesis 18:18: it is God, not the mediator Abraham or his descendants, who is the ultimate source of blessing.[3]

Abraham will neither speak blessings to all the nations, nor embody the entirety of the blessing himself. Rather, God promises to bless those who are on good terms with Abraham. Here *brk* is used in the general sense of "bestow benefits." God initiated the blessing, and God saw it through. He knew the ins and outs that would be revealed. He knew the toll of waiting and the outcome of it all.

The Abrahamic Blessing Promise is an archetype for the blessing of Jesus. God's long-range purpose for issuing the blessing was to bless all peoples. "All the families of the earth shall be blessed" (Genesis 12:3). Note: "all families" or "all nations" shall actually acquire blessing. The coming blessing is pervasive and real. This is not a matter of wishful thinking or swapping the blessings of man: Jesus would take humanity into Himself and be the woman's Seed. God was preparing His salvation before the face of all people, a light to lighten the Gentiles and the glory of God's people Israel.[4]

We won't go through all the narratives of Abraham, but Genesis 17 brings out another purpose for the Abrahamic Blessing. The passage describes God's promises at some length, including the statements "I will make you exceedingly fruitful" and "kings shall come from you" (v. 6). It references the land of Canaan specifically, as well as an everlasting covenant (17:1–8). Then God uses the promise of the blessings of descendants and land to motivate Abraham to accept the covenant of circumcision. God details the blessings (vv. 2–9) before stating the requirements of the covenant (vv. 10–14).

Blessings can

- establish a relationship;
- characterize a relationship;
- be legally binding;
- form alliances;
- praise;
- congratulate;
- motivate;
- be mediated;
- be a resource to share; and
- be conditional.

Additional Blessings

After an eventful time in Egypt—particularly between Pharaoh and Sarai—and Lot's time in Sodom, but before Abram is renamed, Abram is blessed by Melchizedek, "priest of God Most High" (Genesis 14:17–24):

> Blessed be Abram by God Most High,
>   Possessor of heaven and earth;
> and blessed be God Most High,
> who has delivered your enemies into your hand! (vv. 19–20)

As a priest, Melchizedek's blessing does more than thank Abram for expelling their common enemies. As the representative of "God Most High" (El Elyon[5]), he declares that his God is on Abram's side. By giving a tithe, Abram accepts Melchizedek as a legitimate priest and accepts his blessing as authoritative. Melchizedek's blessing congratulates Abram after his victory over the kings of the East.[6]

In Genesis 14:19–20, you can clearly see a parallel construction between Abram and God. Praising Abram functions to praise God and vice versa. This is not at all to imply equality between the two, but it illustrates an interesting point. The blesser/blessed roles are part of a socially recognized relationship.

The blesser aligns himself with the blessed. Elsewhere in Scripture, one comes across "blessing" as a request to enter into an alliance or treaty.[7] Praising Abram, or praising the God of Abram, serves to praise the other also, precisely in recognizing that it is *God* "who has delivered your enemies into your hand!" (Genesis 14:20).[8]

Sarai receives a specific blessing in Genesis 17:15–16, after she tried to take matters into her own hands through arranging an additional marriage for her husband. Although one can infer her to be included in the blessing in Abram's blessing in Genesis 12:1–3, given the Genesis teaching on the one-flesh union in marriage, in Genesis 17 our Lord spells it out explicitly to Abram, now renamed Abraham. Sarai, now Sarah, is to have a son. She is to be blessed. She shall become nations, and kings of peoples shall come from her.

Her blessing, one might note, does not contain the refrain about mediating blessing and curse. On one hand, if she is included as a mediator in Abraham's initial blessing, perhaps that is why the Lord allows Abraham to divorce Hagar according to Sarah's demand. On the other hand, she may be excluded. It certainly would have been problematic if she were to curse Ishmael, whom God promised to make into a great nation (Genesis 16:10; 17:20; 21:17–18).

Interestingly, Sarah's blessing is not given directly to her at all, only to her husband. Hers is a mediated blessing, passed from husband to wife. On the other hand, when Hagar twice fled Sarah in fear, Ishmael's blessing is given directly to her twice (Genesis 16:7–14; 21:17–18), though it was also given to Abraham (17:20).

Extensions of Abram's Blessing

This initial blessing branches into various elaborations from God at different times. In Genesis 15, we see that Abram is struggling with doubt. God affirms His blessing and throughout the chapter expands it with the description of offspring more numerous than the stars. However, blessings are not all joy and peace. Abram must wait for his own son to be his heir, and Abram's offspring would be "sojourners in a land that is not theirs and will be servants there, and they will be afflicted for four hundred years" (Genesis 15:12–16).

Abram received a powerful promised blessing. Still, his story includes these aspects:

- Lying so that Pharaoh took Sarai as his own
- Lot moving away because of squabbling servants
- Fighting alongside Sodom to retrieve Lot with his people and possessions
- A blessing from Melchizedek
- Fearing his childlessness
- Learning of four hundred years of affliction for his future offspring (Genesis 15:13)
- And then entering a covenant with the Lord (Genesis 15:18)

Blessings do not prevent personal fears, struggles with family, great external needs, war, and long periods of waiting. Rather, "Blessed is the man who takes *refuge* in Him!" (Psalm 34:8, emphasis added).

By blessing the patriarchs, as we call our spiritual forefathers Abraham, Isaac, and Jacob, (Romans 4:15–17), God clearly intended them to be in a relationship of faith toward Him and to acquire fame and renown. The blessing goes even further, promising that others will seek to establish good relationships with the blessed so as to acquire blessing too.

This overflowing blessing did not mean the patriarchs had to take an active role toward others in order to enable any sort of blessing transfer. In Genesis 17:20, God promises to bless Ishmael with the same benefits he promised to Isaac in verse 16: Ishmael will become a great people apart from Abraham and will father rulers. God promises to fulfill some of his promises to Abraham in Ishmael's line simply because he is related to Abraham.

Abraham's covenant with God was to be "in your flesh" (Genesis 17:13). Abraham and the males in his family were to be circumcised—not because human actions or piety saves, but as a sign of the covenant between God and His people (Genesis 17:11). As the apostle Paul says, circumcision is not merely outward and physical (Romans 2:28).

God would provide, and man was to trust. "For what does the Scripture say? 'Abraham believed God, and it was counted to him as righteousness' " (Romans 4:3). And (emphasis added):

> [Abraham] received the sign of circumcision as a seal of the righteousness that he had by faith *while he was still uncircumcised.* The purpose was to make him the father of all who believe without being circumcised, so that righteousness would be counted to them as well, and to make him the father of the circumcised who are not merely circumcised but who also walk in the footsteps of the faith that our father Abraham had before he was circumcised. (Romans 4:11–12)

Paul writes:

> Know then that it is those of faith who are the sons of Abraham. And the Scripture, foreseeing that God would justify the Gentiles by faith, preached the gospel beforehand to Abraham, saying, "In you shall all the nations be blessed." So then, those who are of faith are blessed along with Abraham, the man of faith. (Galatians 3:7–9)

Thanks be to God that Abraham is our father and that God has so greatly blessed us through him! Now Jesus is in our flesh and will always remain so. We rejoice with Abraham, who "rejoiced that he would see [Christ's] day. He saw it and was glad" (John 8:56).

Blessed be the Lord God of Israel,
  for He has visited and redeemed His people
and has raised up a horn of salvation for us
  in the house of His servant David,
as he spoke by the mouth of His holy prophets from of old,
that we should be saved from our enemies
  and from the hand of all who hate us;
to show the mercy promised to our fathers
  and to remember His holy covenant,
the oath that He swore to our father Abraham, to grant us
  that we, being delivered from the hand of our enemies,
might serve Him without fear,
in holiness and righteousness before Him all our days.
(Luke 1:68–75)

CHAPTER 5

Isaac

Genesis 27 is a powerfully insightful passage on blessings as portrayed in Scripture. The scene is set with an old, increasingly blind father seeking to bless his son. During a private moment together, Isaac offers this blessing:

> May God give you of the dew of heaven
> and of the fatness of the earth
> and plenty of grain and wine.
> Let peoples serve you,
> and nations bow down to you.
> Be lord over your brothers,
> and may your mother's sons bow down to you.
> Cursed be everyone who curses you,
> and blessed be everyone who blesses you! (Genesis 27:28–29)

Instead of a divinely revealed blessing by God, a man is blessing his son. This is a human benediction, or pronouncement of good, which asks God to bestow His favor and tangible expressions of that favor. More specifically, this is a testamental blessing. It is distinguished by the occasion and purpose, which is imminent death and a message to one's son(s).

Near the beginning of the narrative, Isaac asks Esau to go hunting and prepare food "such as I love," so that "my soul may bless you before I die" (Genesis 27:4). This is not proof that souls are responsible for blessings, despite suggestions to the contrary. Rather, Isaac's words may be translated "so that I may wholeheartedly bless you."

Then, when the time for blessing has come, Isaac exclaims: "See, my son's smell is like the smell of a field, which Yahweh has blessed" (Genesis 27:27 CM). This is the form of *brk* that means to thrive.

That field may also serve as a bridge into the blessing. When Isaac asks God for his son to be blessed with water and well-pastured animals, it calls to mind the field that so perfumed Esau—and Jacob's costume. Perhaps Isaac tailored his blessing to Esau's strengths: "a skillful hunter, a man of the field" (Genesis 25:27).

Of course, the rich imagery of "dew of heaven" and "fatness of the earth" draws upon prosperity. Considering once more the Hebrew expression "Do not destroy [the cluster of grapes], for there is a blessing in it" (Isaiah 65:8), we see how extensive it was for Isaac to seek the dew of heaven for his son.

Isaac calls upon God to bless with a range literally from heaven to earth. Note the deep, ongoing appreciation for the physical, for creation and God's blessings set within it. There is no hint of later-developing Gnosticism. Isaac literally wants the world for his son.

Plenty of grain and wine round out the blessing, adding more cultivated elements. The very generous, inclusive inheritance speaks of ample God-given water, pastoral farming (pastured animals), arable farming (cultivated crops), and either easy trade or a fully functioning winery (both vineyard and press)!

Whether all these symbols and sources of prosperity exchanged hands is not said, but the blessing is remarkably thorough. The climax invokes the Abrahamic (or Patriarchal) Blessing by including "let peoples serve you," "be lord over your brothers," and "blessed be everyone who blesses you!" (Genesis 27:29).

The Lord blesses Jacob through Isaac with such certainty that later texts refer to God's promises to Abraham, Isaac, and Jacob. This strongly affirms the continuity of blessing between the patriarchs. It also calls to mind the specific stories of blessing and God's merciful favor upon each of them.

Esau

The plot thickens. There is a second son, indeed the firstborn son who had expected the blessing. He walks through the door moments after his brother leaves, having obediently fulfilled what his father requested of him. Together, Isaac and Esau learn of Jacob's deception.

We expect a quick "Bless me too!" but Esau's response far exceeds that. "He cried out with an exceedingly great and bitter cry and said to his father, 'Bless me, even me also. . . . Have you not reserved a blessing for me?" (Genesis 27:34, 36). Without a moment's hesitation, Esau recognized that Isaac's blessing of Jacob would continue to stand.

It is because blessings are more than words that Isaac "trembled very violently" (v. 33). The deceiver remained the recipient of his final blessing. Isaac goes so far as to say:

" 'Behold, I have made him lord over you, and all his brothers I have given to him for servants, and with grain and wine I have sustained him. What then can I do for you, my son?' Esau said to his father, 'Have you but one blessing, my father? Bless me, even me also, O my father.' And Esau lifted up his voice and wept."

> Then Isaac his father answered and said to him:
> "Behold, away from the fatness of the earth shall your dwelling be,
> and away from the dew of heaven on high.
> By your sword you shall live,
> and you shall serve your brother;
> but when you grow restless
> you shall break his yoke from your neck." (27:37–40)

The heartbreak is palpable and the manipulation so apparent. Rebekah and Jacob hid behind the weakness of Isaac's eyes to open his mouth in blessing. How did the ruse come together so quickly? Rebekah cooked, and Jacob costumed. In shocking deception, Jacob answered his father's surprise, saying, "Because the Lord your God granted me success" (Genesis 27:20).

In fatherly devotion, Isaac answered Esau. He gives what was not given to Jacob: a sword. And although he will be a servant to Jacob, eventually Esau will "grow restless" and "break his yoke."

Clearly, blessings are not merely wishful thinking, even when a person does it. How was such an inexcusable scenario permitted to stand? Why did everyone involved presume that God would uphold such an unintended blessing?

Human Power

Some scholars have argued that Isaac transferred his own soul power to his son during the blessing and thereby lacked the strength to undo it. The meal, they speculate, was necessary fuel for the exchange. Such lengths to imagine man as the power within blessing! A festive family meal, a favorite tasty morsel, gets painted as a pagan spell rather than Isaac simply wanting a delicious meal from Esau in pride of his son's skills.

Variations on that misconception can include belief that one's strengths or excellence, often in prayer, impact how well your blessings bless. Or passion and emotional strength are seen to convey the blessing. Can momentary conviction deny the possibility of change?

A more common perspective, reading Genesis 27, is to inquire into intent. Isn't intent related to blessing? Isn't intent a force behind it?

This passage strongly challenges that notion. Isaac's intentions are directly thwarted. In a very literal sense, Isaac's blessing did the opposite of what he meant to do: he took from Esau and gave to Jacob. He sought to bless Esau mightily and categorically failed.

If your only intention is to express goodwill or warmth toward a person, saying "Bless you" can accomplish that. However it is not human intent, focus, or imagined outcomes that ultimately direct blessings. It is not one's soul or one's wholeheartedness that sets things into motion. In the instance of Genesis 27, it was words, not because of any innate "soul power" invested within them, but because God listens.

Words are powerful. Some scholars have argued that blessings and curses have self-fulfilling power. Speak and make it so. Name and claim. Still, it is telling—and defying—that Scripture used in such arguments (for example Genesis 1; Jeremiah 1:9–10; Isaiah 55:10–11) are descriptive of God's Word rather than words themselves.

Words are powerful things, but haven't we all been denied things we ask for? Haven't we all experienced that drop of our stomach when something agreed upon—and counted on—falls through? Human words simply do not have the power of God's words.

Of course, both divine and human words communicate. Both can warn or promise. Both can self-reveal. They reflect relationship and the nuance of a given situation. Words teach, request, suggest, thank, demand, promise, warn, and much more. Sadly, words do not always mean there is understanding.

Blessings in Scripture often use words, or are at least revealed to us by words, so we need to take into account the powers, flexibility, and uses for them, as well as the functions and abilities of the specific words we are considering.

Both can be legally binding. That is what "forensic justification" is about: God's verdict of "not guilty" because the punishment of sin has already been borne by Christ in our stead.

Context matters. If a child says "Not guilty," no prisoner walks free. If those same words are spoken in a socially recognized fashion, by the proper person and in the right form, the courthouse doors open wide. A judge's verdict is powerful and effective.

At the same time, that verdict is not a personal decree. It is not a demonstration of the judge's inner powers. It is wholly dependent upon external factors. The judge has been placed into his position and granted the authority or power to give a verdict: it does not come from within him or from a mere ability to speak.

Human words do not inevitably bring about whatever is said, but they are endowed with the ability to communicate, linking together individuals, societies, and even God to man. Words are no substitute for deeds (Proverbs 14:23); words cannot alter facts (Proverbs 26:23–28; 28:24); and words cannot compel a response. They are ineffective if the person addressed does not understand them, and sometimes even if he does (Proverbs 2:3–4; 17:4, 10; 29:19).

Still, ours is a God who speaks and listens. Ours is a world with language natural to it. Words matter and do have power, as do other elements involved.

In academic circles, one way to describe the power of words is through discussing force. *Perlocutionary* force tries to affect other people. Whether they seek to console, persuade, frighten, assure, request, or demand, some words are spoken primarily to affect individuals more than situations.

The force most common in blessing language is *illocutionary.* That means the words themselves *do* something. Sometimes called a "performative utterance," these words accomplish an action. For example, "I swear," puts a person under oath: it changes the situation. "Help!" requests. "Stop!" warns. Other examples of illocutionary speech acts are promises, the act of naming, legal declarations, and oral blessings and curses.

> Illocutionary = performed by speaking, i.e.,
> God's "Let there be" creates.
> Perlocutionary = producing an effect by speaking, i.e.,
> "Let's eat there" suggests.

The two forces are not mutually exclusive. When a person says "thank you," he thereby give thanks (the illocutionary force) and attempts to make the other person feel appreciated (the perlocutionary force). Similarly, blessings and curses, though illocutionary statements are often pronounced in order to affect the recipient in some way.

All of this is to say that blessings, as language, are both illocutionary and perlocutionary. God's Word performs what it says, and God's Word produces an effect. Blessings recorded in Scripture have a secondary effect by continuing to reveal God's love and deeds: they continue to impact us.

Although we are right to look for the efficacious, powerful Word of God in Scripture, we go too far when we seek it in the words of man, even those recorded in the Bible. Circumstances involving God speaking to a prophet, or instruction from an apostle, fall into a more honored category. That God chooses to work through human words is a profound and humbling thing, but a close reading of Scripture—seeking things such as the speaker and with whom he is speaking—offer us external clues for the sake of discernment.

The strength of words, in the case of inclusion into Scripture, is that performative speech is valid only when spoken by the proper person. Performative speech performs the word spoken: a judge's "not guilty" releases; God's "Let there be . . ." makes. But you know how the

Book of Job includes long stretches of human speculation that at times urges Job to curse God and die? That is *not* performative speech, even though it is included in Scripture. The speaker and scenario matter.

The difference between a false prophet or teacher, and a true prophet or teacher, lies with God. Society and itching ears (2 Timothy 4:3) may hear words and choose their preference between them, but fallen humanity isn't very discerning. Even Christians are warned to trust neither princes (Psalm 146:3) nor their own understanding (Proverbs 3:5) and to test the spirits and their spiritual teachers (1 John 4:1).

This brings us full circle. Although human words can certainly put things into motion, the ultimate power behind words lies with God.

Binding Words

When individuals bless, they invoke what is external to them. Isaac called upon God to provide, and there was no thought of renegotiating.

When Isaac offers his testamental blessing—as in last will and testament—in Genesis 27, this is a prime example of an illocutionary speech act. His words are accomplishing something. In short, he gave his word in a way that was legally binding.

One way that the speech was set apart from other conversations is the formulaic expression "I have grown old," as seen in 27:2 (CM). That expression could be compared to other traditional introductions to a will, such as, "I, being of sound mind and body, do hereby declare."

Isaac issued an oral disposition of his estate in the form of a blessing.

A discovery known as the Nuzi tablets provides archaeological evidence and support of this tradition. Nuzi was a provincial town in ancient Mesopotamia, located near the Tigris River. According to Dr. Bryant Wood, the Hurrians are equivalent to the Horites in the Old Testament and are also called Hivites and Jebusites.[1]

During archaeological excavations spanning from 1925 to 1933, more than five thousand tablets were found dealing with social, economic, religious, and legal matters, spanning six generations. These tablets demonstrate practices similar to several narratives in Genesis.[2]

For our purposes, one Nuzi lawsuit introduced his father's deathbed testament as evidence in a trial. The plaintiff quotes the testament verbatim, and though the testament was never written down, the judge rules that the final oral disposition by the head of a household had solid legal standing.[3]

Further, it seems that "firstborn" is not necessarily as literal as it seems. Several Nuzi tablets, which granted are certainly not biblical or Hebrew in nature but which demonstrate wider area practices, decreed someone else to the legal status of firstborn, with its double share of the inheritance. When Isaac gave the majority of his inheritance to Jacob, the father's decree legally altered who was deemed firstborn in status.

This may add a bit of context to Jacob's pursuit of Esau's birthright in Genesis 25:29–34, as well as the activity in Genesis 27. And we should not overlook that God had revealed prophetically at their birth that "the older shall serve the younger" (Genesis 25:23).

As deceitful as Jacob was, he was chosen to be in the line and lineage of God Himself. And well we should note that, while Jacob could deceive to obtain a human blessing, he did not wrestle one from God. Instead, God kept His word of prophecy that "two nations are in [Rebekah's] womb, and two peoples from within [her] shall be divided; the one shall be stronger than the other, the older shall serve the younger" (Genesis 25:23).

Obviously, the blessing has legal as well as religious significance. Isaac called upon God as the one who bestows blessings; through the blessing, Jacob inherits. More than money and an honored position, Jacob gained the Abrahamic Blessing, the most remarkable legacy in the history of salvation (Genesis 26:2–5)! Only Christ's eternal inheritance in heaven compares!

> Blessings can be highly ritualized and bear a legal component. They can also be tied to prophecies, as every blessing is fulfilled according to God's timing.

Natural Processes

Though God has blessed by bestowing power directly upon people, God usually blesses through the natural processes. There is no good biblical evidence for a *Segenskraft,* a power distinct from God through which blessing is bestowed. Human blessings never transfer power to other people or to God. Human blessings often simply express the speaker's sentiments and do not make the recipient acquire material goods.

A father blesses his son, and the Lord listens. The Lord indeed blesses the man, despite his many shortcomings. God takes the man and makes him the head of a family that would bless all peoples and every nation throughout time. God showered earthly goods upon him and sent not only dew from heaven but the Bread from heaven into his bloodline.

Although for us, the fatness of the earth, grain, and wine may conjure images of a hearty good time, they can also turn us to consider the sacrifices the Israelites offered to God. Offering up what God first gave to them, the Israelites looked to God for atonement based on His promise to look with favor upon them.

Christ is the perfect sacrifice and atonement. In Him, we are left with sacrifices of praise and thanksgiving. In Him, we have both ceremonial cleanliness and "our hearts sprinkled clean from an evil conscience and our bodies washed with pure water" (Hebrews 10:22), cleansed from all sin and unrighteousness (1 John 1:7–9).

In Jesus, we may not have nations bowing down to us (an illocutionary application of Jacob's blessing), but we are included in the promise that all nations will bow to Him (a perlocutionary effect). And not only is Christ Lord "over your brothers," but He makes us to be His brothers, drawing us into His own flesh and family.

CHAPTER 6

The Patriarchal Blessing Promises

Abraham's blessing was passed down and became Isaac's and Jacob's. In the Patriarchal Blessing Promises, blessings consist of God's bestowal of descendants, fame, dominion over others, land, and God's presence and protection. In addition, God's blessing also consists of the conferral of the status of mediator of blessing upon the patriarchs.

This was a type of inheritance far different from a family possession or heirloom, which people could pass on independently of God. This was an ongoing, living, fleshly act of God for the sake of every family since Adam and Eve. Their very lives would have a serious impact on those around them, precisely because God set His favor upon them.

Blessing is not some contagious, mysterious power that a man who is blessed possesses and exudes onto others. Jacob did not personally make Laban's herds thrive; he simply possessed the blessings God bestowed on him. Genesis 30:27, 30 clearly state that it is the Lord who has the power to bless. Since God promised to bless Jacob, both Jacob and Laban could expect God to bless their shared undertaking.

Joseph mediated blessing in a similar way. Potiphar appointed Joseph as manager of his household and,

> From the time that he made him overseer in his house and over all that he had, the Lord blessed the Egyptian's house for Joseph's sake; the blessing of the Lord was on all that he had, in house and field. (Genesis 39:5)

The phrase "the blessing of the LORD" is equivalent in meaning to the preceding phrase "the LORD blessed." This describes God in the activity of blessing. God's blessing here does not consist of a force or of another entity, but of an *activity.*

Blessing alongside Suffering

Although the pious may be quick to say, "God stayed with Joseph during his captivity," they may be less quick to recognize that God entered into his very suffering. It was in the midst of great scandal and abuse—including domestic physical abuse, workplace sexual harassment, and the abject status as slave—that God provided for both Joseph and the future of Israel.

Our Lord looked with favor on Abram and Sarai in the state of their barrenness. He looked with favor on Joseph in his state of prisoner and slave. God answered the needs of all of them, but He did not do so through instant liberation or multiple children. He did so by providing Himself. He gave His Word, His blessing, and His benevolent presence as He prepared to fulfill His promises to them and the world in Jesus, His perfect and only Son. Of course, He entered into earthly suffering too, taking the form of a servant, humble and obedient to the point of death, even death on a cross.

> God's favor and God's presence go hand in hand. God's blessings are not removed from Him, but they enter into our very own circumstances with the grace and mercy of Jesus Christ.

As the blessing formula becomes thematic within the Old Testament, descendants are the most frequently mentioned blessing. God promises to make Abram into a great nation (Genesis 12:2; 17:16, 20; 18:18) and to give the patriarchs numerous descendants (22:17; 26:4; 28:14). In 17:16, 20, God further promises to make some of the descendants into rulers.

God's presence, i.e., being with the patriarchs (26:3, 24; 28:15, 20) is a general expression denoting God's benefaction and favorable disposition toward the one he is "with." Remember that far from a tepid platitude, this would remind the people that God is as much with them in battle as in childbirth and daily life.

God's blessing presence, then, is another way of saying God's saving presence. When God turns His favor upon someone, it elicits mercy and reconciliation according to the covenant, the Abrahamic Covenant that encompasses all people, drawing to mind Jesus, the height of Abraham's pride.

In Genesis 28:15, God promises to reveal His presence by protecting Jacob: "Behold, I am with you and will guard you . . . I will not forsake you" (CM; similarly, Joshua 1:5; Psalm 37:24; 2 Corinthians 4:9). Our Lord likewise reveals His presence in Christ through the Word: "Behold, I am with you always, to the end of the age" (Matthew 28:20).

Blessing includes dominion over others in Genesis 12:3a; 18:18; 22:17, where God says, "I will certainly bless you . . . and so your descendants will take possession of their enemies' gate" (CM). Dominion is also implied in the promise of land, since it must be conquered. God promises land in conjunction with blessing in 12:1; 26:3–4; 28:13. (See also the Covenantal Blessing.)

Fame is promised explicitly only in 12:2, but it is implied in many of the other promises. The blessings of dominion and being a mediator of blessing, for example, would certainly bring prestige and renown.

Israel indeed enjoyed fame and benefited from it. Consider Rahab's confession as she hid the two Israelite spies sent into Jericho:

> I know that the Lord has given you the land, and that the fear of you has fallen upon us, and that all the inhabitants of the land melt away before you. For we have heard how the Lord dried up the water of the Red Sea before you when you came out of Egypt, and what you did to the two kings of the Amorites who were beyond the Jordan, to Sihon and Og, whom you devoted to destruction. And as soon as we heard it, our hearts melted, and there was no spirit left in any man because of you, for the Lord your God, He is God in the heavens above and on the earth beneath. (Joshua 2:9–11)

The Lord was acting publicly for the sake of His people, and the Canaanites knew it. Following God's victory at Jericho, Joshua's fame spread throughout the land (Joshua 6:27).

Still, fame does not seem to be of primary significance. This is one aspect promised to the faithful Israelites that is no longer reflected in the New Testament. Although some fame accumulated around Jesus during His earthly ministry, fame is not, as some would hope, considered to be a mark (or sign) of the Church.[1] After all, Jesus said within the most famous list of blessings, the Beatitudes, "Blessed are you when others revile you and persecute you and utter all kinds of evil against you falsely on My account" (Matthew 5:11). Also:

> If you were of the world, the world would love you as its own; but because you are not of the world, but I chose you out of the world, therefore the world hates you. Remember the word that I said to you: "A servant is not greater than his master." If they persecuted Me, they will also persecute you. If they kept My word, they will also keep yours. (John 15:19–20)

Martin Luther draws upon Matthew 5 in explaining the seventh mark of the Church: the sacred cross. He goes so far as to say:

> [The holy Christian people] must endure every misfortune and persecution, all kinds of trials and evil from the devil, the world, and the flesh (as the Lord's Prayer indicates) by inward sadness, timidity, fear, outward poverty, contempt, illness, and weakness, in order to become like their head, Christ. . . . Wherever you see or hear this, you may know that the holy Christian church is there, as Christ says in Matthew 5 [:11–12], "*Blessed are you when men revile you and utter all kinds of evil against you on my account* [emphasis added]. Rejoice and be glad, for your reward is great in heaven." This, too, is a holy possession whereby the Holy Spirit not only sanctifies his people, but also blesses them.[2]

The Holy Spirit blesses you when you carry the burdens of your daily cross, even when that cross includes persecution or cultural marginalization because of Christ.

Diachronic Blessing

Diachronic means "through time." The Patriarchal Blessings are unique in that they are transmitted diachronically. That is, sometimes God added descriptions over time, but moreover He actually renews His promises of blessing to each patriarch. God specifies that Isaac's line will carry on the covenant that He made with Abraham (17:16–21).

God assures Isaac, "I will bless you and make your descendants numerous for the sake of Abraham My servant" (Genesis 26:24 CM; cf. 26:3–4 and the promise to Jacob in 28:13–15). "For the sake of Abraham" becomes a major, ongoing theme, explaining why God is so slow to anger with His people, despite their waywardness.

The reason the Patriarchal Blessings were transmitted diachronically is that they were still *promises* and were not completely fulfilled in the lifetime of the original recipients. Other types of blessing promises could not be passed on, but God was insistent with the Abrahamic Blessing: the Christ would come through that flesh-and-blood family.

Promises

When children first begin to realize that their parents do not always keep their words, there is one thing they seek: a promise. They want to trust words again, and a promise seems to them to be an extra level of security. If parents promise, there is extra incentive to keep their word. To be fair, parents turn to promises too. "Do you promise to . . . " do any number of things, because we very much want to trust our children. We want them to be mindful and safe.

Promises, in a sense, are a sad thing. In a perfect world, there would be no need to promise. Our word would be our oath. We would do what we say, and no shortcomings or stumbling—or grievances or temptations—would dilute or squander our love or relationships.

On the other hand, what was the kindest, gentlest thing God could do for us when He spoke to Adam and Eve? After Adam and Eve each turned away from the Word of God, He spoke again, this time with a promise.

It was not the warm, feel-good kind of promise many in our society would expect. It was actually something of a fierce promise spoken to the serpent himself:

> Because you have done this,
> cursed are you above all livestock
> and above all beasts of the field;
> on your belly you shall go,
> and dust you shall eat
> all the days of your life.
> I will put enmity between you and the woman,
> and between your offspring and her offspring;
> He shall bruise your head,
> and you shall bruise His heel. (Genesis 3:14–15)

The ground is cursed. Adam must toil and sweat; woman's pain would be multiplied in childbearing, and her desire would be for her husband, who would rule over her. Shame had entered their life. Death would come for them all. They had known, and chosen, evil, and they were no longer to reach out and eat from the tree of life (Genesis 3:16–24). Still, Satan's curse becomes our blessing.

Sometimes, the enemy of your enemy is your friend. When God put enmity between the serpent and the woman, our God also revealed whose side He is on: ours! The enmity between the devil and man is enmity between the devil and the Son who became man.

Also note in the next verse that the man called his wife's name Eve (Genesis 3:20). She would be the mother of all the living. The deceiver would be brought down, and the woman would still bear children. Life would continue, and God would enter into man's newfound fight against the devil.

The Lord God covered their nakedness and shame. Moreover, He was still speaking to them!

God promised, albeit while cursing Satan, because He still turned in favor to Adam and Eve. He would bless them in their newfound need for forgiveness, life, and salvation. He would send His Son into the world, under the Law, and into their suffering and need as woman's Seed to conquer sin, death, and the power of the devil.

In Genesis 3:15, God's Word became a promise, and as God repeatedly turned in favor to mankind, who needs Him so desperately, He continued according to that promise. He continued to speak and give His Word, and He added the depth, comfort, and enticement to trust by His promise.

The majority of God's blessings are promises. Some were fulfilled more quickly than others, such as prophecies completed within the lifetime of the hearers. Some promises are given corporately, yet fulfilled by some and not others (hence, fertility is a blessing, but infertility is not a lack of blessing)—but every word and every promise points to the larger reality of Jesus Christ, incarnate, crucified, and raised in love and mercy toward us.

God's promises are expressions of blessing.

As Christians, when we think of God's promises, we likely think about His promise to send a Savior and His promise to take us to heaven to be with Him. We may think about His promise to work through His Word and His promise to be with us always. Old Testament academics consider God's promises to David and the prophets and, of course, the many blessing promises. Linguistic academics, however, have wondered about the relationship between blessings and deliverance, since deliverance is such a dominating theme in the Old Testament. Some scholars have suggested a more narrow view of blessing, speculating that perhaps God blesses through natural processes, but that He delivers by supernatural, or miraculous, events. Such a suggestion separates blessing from deliverance and salvation.

There certainly are large differences, both in the range of meaning and in the range of application, between *brk* and the words of deliverance; however, blessing and deliverance, or salvation, are not so widely divided.

Deliverance

In Exodus 6, God promises to deliver the Israelites from slavery in Egypt. Exodus 6:2–3, 8 specifically connect God's actions on behalf of Israel with the patriarchs and His promise to them.

Although the subsequent exodus is not preceded by an immediate, explicit blessing, it does directly correspond to God's blessing to Abram and his offspring. Within God's elaboration of Abram's blessing in Genesis 15:13, we hear the prediction that Abram's offspring will be afflicted for four hundred years. Such a prediction presupposes both suffering and deliverance, yet God's blessing maintains the overriding feature for Abram and presumably for those who rejoiced in his blessing.

Such a connection between the Abrahamic Blessing and the archetypes of deliverance—the exodus from Egypt and the conquest of Canaan—demonstrates not only a unified intention by Him who blesses and delivers but also God acting in favor toward recipients of His gifts. Indeed, given that blessing is so closely associated with the favorable presence and action of God, the deliverance or victory of every battle may rightly be ascribed to God and His blessing. In Exodus 23:20–33, God's blessing activity (v. 25) is an integral part of God enabling Israel to conquer Canaan, and Balaam recognizes that Israel is blessed (Numbers 22:12), because God is delivering her from Egypt (23:22; 24:8).

God blessed Samson to enable him to deliver Israel (Judges 13:24–25). In Scripture, God both blesses to deliver and delivers to bless. He offers peace and rescue.

In passages reciting God's beneficent deeds, such as Psalms 106; 107; and Nehemiah 9:5–31, God's acts of blessing are listed alongside His acts of deliverance. Within their context, there is no indication that the two represent separate types of God's activity.

The root *brk* occurs in deliverance contexts in Isaiah 19:24–25; 44:3; 61:9; 65:23; Ezekiel 34:26; Zechariah 8:13. Blessing is equated with deliverance also in Psalms 3:8; 21:6 (cf. v. 4); 28:9; 67:7 (cf. v. 2); 109:26b, 31b (cf. v. 28a).

Land and dominion are additional connections. Land in particular is one of the most important benefits of the Patriarchal Blessing

Promises. Many passages promise the land as a result of God's blessing, drawing together the conquest of Canaan with the promised blessing, the Promised Land. Likewise, the blessing theme of dominion/victory is indistinguishable from deliverance. Though dominion is never the sole element of God's blessing, it is a major element in blessings in Genesis 1:28–30; 9:1–3; 12:3; 22:17; 27:29; Exodus 23:20–33; Deuteronomy 7:14–18; 15:6; 28:1; 33:11.

Even Genesis 3:15 connects delivery with blessing. Eve would be blessed through her Seed with one who would crush the serpent's head; this would not be a matter of simple vengeance, but of deliverance.

Salvation

"Let Your steadfast love come to me, O LORD, Your salvation according to Your promise. . . . My eyes long for Your salvation and for the fulfillment of Your righteous promise" (Psalm 119:41, 123). "Behold, now is the favorable time; behold, now is the day of salvation" (2 Corinthians 6:2).

In the Patriarchal Blessing, we see the continuation of God's mercy to Adam and Eve and His intention to bless all mankind through *family.* Blessing, deliverance, and salvation become personal through Abram, Sarai, and their kin. This is divine anticipation of the Son entering the womb of a Hebrew maiden of the tribe of Judah in the line of Abram. And even now, we have His promises in Scripture—His Good News—sustaining us: promises we share with each subsequent generation and with whomever we can.

Many verses explicitly tie God's blessing activity to His love for or favor toward man using expressions such as love, shining, loving kindness, or steadfast love—even beyond the obligations of the covenant—and delight to describe God's attitude toward the person(s) blessed.[3]

In Psalms 24:5; 112:3b (cf. v. 2b; cf. also Deuteronomy 24:13), God's blessing is equated with *tsedaqah,* covenantal righteousness itself. That is to say, God's blessing includes God's legal verdict of "righteous" pronounced upon the person blessed. That is forensic justification—being made right with God—the bedrock of Lutheranism and our understanding of faith. "For what does the Scripture say? 'Abraham believed God, and it was counted to him as righteousness' " (Romans 4:3).

While we go through our toil, troubles, and trials, we can depend on God to keep His promises: we await fulfillment when Jesus comes again. God desires to bring the peoples to Himself. He desires to bless, and He desires to bless through the free gift of His only-begotten Son, very God of very God.

How does He reach out? He reaches out with His Word and promises pointing to His Son and His mercy. He grants forgiveness of sins, cover for shame, and provision for rest. "Blessed be the Lord who has given rest to His people Israel, according to all that He promised. Not one word has failed of all His good promise, which He spoke by Moses His servant" (1 Kings 8:56). Thanks be to God.

Conditional Covenantal Blessing

Exodus tells the great account of the Israelite captivity in Egypt, their exodus, the Sinai Covenant, and the crafting of the tabernacle. Moses faces Pharaoh, leads Israel, and speaks face-to-face with God. Turning to the Book of Deuteronomy, we find all the Israelites are gathered. Many battles—and forty years in the wilderness—are behind them. They are on the verge of entering the land long promised to them, and the great Moses delivers his final sermon.

Moses reminds them of their God and their rebellion. He "undertook to explain this law" (Deuteronomy 1:5),[1] and he spoke at length about blessing and curses.

They were standing at the edge of partial fulfillment of the Patriarchal Promise. For so long, they longed for numbers, strength, and land, and now their time had come. But while there was little to do but grumble and follow God in the wilderness, there would be additional temptation in Canaan, particularly regarding the false gods.

There are many allusions to the Abrahamic Blessing, as well as the patriarchal forms. In the first chapter, Moses says:

> Go in and take possession of the land that the LORD swore to your fathers, to Abraham, to Isaac, and to Jacob, to give to them and to their offspring after them. . . . The LORD your God has multiplied you, and behold, you are today as numerous as the stars of heaven. May the LORD, the God of your fathers, make you a thousand times as many as you are and bless you, as He has promised you! (Deuteronomy 1:8, 10–11)

Israel is given a choice: blessing or curse. Moses outlines the two options available for them and lets them decide which course they will follow, reminiscent of both the "two ways" theme in the Wisdom Literature and Jesus' declaration of divinity, "I am the way" (John 14:6). Blessing and curse depict two contrasting ways of life: in God's favor and against God's favor.

The Covenantal Blessing, reaching back to Mount Sinai and the Ten Commandments, is built around and based on the Abrahamic Blessing. It is because God reached out in merciful blessing to a single man that God continually reached out to the Israelites. However, unlike that unconditional foundation, there were conditions for God to reside among them (Exodus 29:45; Leviticus 26:45). The blessings and curses reveal the strength of God's conditions (26:46).[2]

As in the patriarchal narratives, God's blessing consisted of human fertility (Exodus 23:26; Deuteronomy 7:13–14; 28:4, 11; 30:16), but, as He is addressing a group of people rather than the direct bloodline of Christ, God does not promise that the descendants will be rulers or mediators of blessing. Moses tells the people that if they obey the covenant, "you will live long and be numerous and the Lord our God will bless you on the land to which you are traveling to inherit" (Deuteronomy 30:16 CM). Furthermore, in Exodus 19:5–6, God commissions Israel to be a "kingdom of priests and a holy nation," calling to mind God's promises concerning Abraham's seed in Genesis 12:3, 22:18; 26:4 and mediating blessing to all.

The inheritance metaphor takes on an especially poignant image when we remember that none of the previous generation were allowed to enter the Promised Land and the Israelites were listening to Moses for the last time. As much as their faith rested in the God of their fathers, they were a young people. The promise of an inheritance in a new land was a personal and gripping hope.

God promises, "You shall serve the Lord your God, and He will bless your bread and your water, and I will take sickness away from among you. None shall miscarry or be barren in your land; I will fulfill the number of your days" (Exodus 23:25–26). As the people transition from nomadic life to farm and city settlements, God would still provide for His people. The richness of the land would be reflected within the family, and God's blessings would be evident in both work and family.

Deuteronomy 15:4–6 combines dominion and prosperity:

> There will be no poor among you; for the LORD will bless you in the land that the LORD your God is giving you for an inheritance to possess—if only you will strictly obey the voice of the LORD your God, being careful to do all this commandment that I command you today. For the LORD your God will bless you, as He promised you, and you shall lend to many nations, but you shall not borrow, and you shall rule over many nations, but they shall not rule over you.[3]

Purposes

Although the Covenantal Blessing builds upon the preexisting Abrahamic Blessing, the purposes are different. God does not need to reintroduce Himself: His repeated forgiveness and dramatic displays of rescue and provision are evident recent history. He is not approaching a man about blessing all nations; God approaches a nation to establish them as His holy people (Exodus 19:6; Deuteronomy 7:6; 26:19; 28:9), a people whom He values a great deal (Deuteronomy 7:6; 26:18), with whom He dwells (Exodus 29:45; Leviticus 26:45).

God wants them to walk in *His* ways rather than in the ways of the fallen world. He establishes laws for them to obey and observe, and He instructs them to trust His Word "lest [their] heart be deceived, and [they] turn aside and serve other gods and worship them" (Deuteronomy 11:16).

Entering the Promised Land marked a shift in God's relationship with His people. How would a people, once led by promise, respond to partial fulfillment? Faith is unseen; what happens when partial sight is given?

God establishes that He is a God of blessing. Wherever He is present, people receive blessing. God also seeks to associate His previous activities with blessing. By making places associated with His action into places of blessing, He reminds His followers that His previous actions intentionally bring blessings. He says, "In every place where I cause My name to be remembered I will come to you and bless you" (Exodus 20:24).

Why do congregations typically worship in one place? Because it has been a place of blessing that continues to be associated with the presence of Him from whom all blessings flow. God designates centers of worship as primary places where blessing is mediated to the people.

Of course, in the Old Testament, God did not want multiple centers of worship. He desired to dwell among them in a single, visible way. His glory filled the temple (2 Chronicles 7:1, 3; Ezekiel 43:1–5; 44:4). He kept His presence visible by a pillar of cloud by day and a pillar of fire by night until He settled first in the tabernacle and then in the temple. That is, until Jesus "tabernacled" within His mother and then promised to dwell with us always.

Dominion in the Name of the Lord

The blessing given to the Israelites may strike us as rather odd, particularly its emphasis on dominating the Canaanites. It is uncommon at this point in American history to emphasize authority and dominion. But rather than elaborating on the patriarchal theme of mediation, the Covenantal Blessing Promises emphasize a different focal point: one must have in order to share. Israel would be given dominion over other nations in order to share God's blessing.

Dominion can be a negative word. Considering that *dominus* is Latin for Lord may assuage some of the more common fears. Likewise, building upon the generous blessings of the Abrahamic Promise toward all nations, the patriarchal examples of the mediation of blessing (Genesis 18:16–33; 30:27–30; 39:1–6; and the rest of the Joseph narrative; cf. Genesis 21:22–34; 26:23–31) show that the Israelites could mediate blessing only when they themselves enjoyed abundant blessings. Dominion was to be a position of God-given authority over those to whom they mediated blessing.

Authority is another word that elicits mixed responses. Authority in Scripture does not mean tyranny. Jesus Himself explains the term in Mark 10:42–45 as a position for the sake of service. Christians can also be reassured by the teaching of Matthew 28:18: All authority in heaven and on earth has been given to the Son of God.

A significant purpose of the covenantal promises is to motivate the Israelites to continue to observe the stipulations of the covenant already made. Our Lord does not give dominion and authority for abuse, but to share God's gifts in an orderly way. As Paul reminds us: there is order in creation (1 Timothy 2:13). Law serves functions for both individuals and society.

How we treat one another is serious business. How we respond to God likewise can be a matter of life or death. That God gave commands during the conquest of Canaan to destroy entire cities highlights just how serious idolatry is.[4]

The triune God wants man to live in faith toward Him. He wants man to have loving dominion over creation and, under forms of headship such as husband, father, and governor, to have loving, serving lives within society. Hence, He provides different types of law for the sake of fallen and blinded self-control, the human propensity toward idolatry and disorder, and societal regulations. But the purpose of His blessings remains to bring all nations to praise Him as their God.

Then why have conditions? Why temper gift with the potential of its loss?

Conditions

Within the blesser/blessed relationship, the giver is a real, autonomous entity. Remember, the common feature of all the meanings of *brk* is that blessing, whether it consists of a speech act (benediction) or a physical act (benefaction), is an act freely performed that expresses the grace and goodwill of the blesser.

The one thing a blesser cannot do is look with favor at what is personally disdained. God does not support what He opposes. A house divided against itself is not able to stand (Mark 3:25), and every kingdom divided against itself is laid waste (Matthew 12:25; Luke 11:17).

The existence of conditional blessings demonstrates that God does not look equally favorably upon the full spectrum of possibilities. What we do, think, and say is simply not always favorable.

The covenant contains conditions that temper the offered blessings with the potential loss or absence of those blessings. "Conditions" is rarely a favored word—who among us seeks out conditions? Yet we can understand it as a legal term in the setting of a covenant. This covenant is a form of vassal treaty. As a vassal, Israel owed its Lord exclusive loyalty.

The Israelites agreed to comply with the covenantal stipulations and be blessed or to suffer the consequences if they did not comply. The covenant was a legal arrangement entered into by willing partners. By pronouncing the "amen," the people put themselves under the force of the formulas (Deuteronomy 27:15–26).

The Covenantal Blessing Promise emphasizes that the blessing relationship is a two-way street. God promises to maintain His role as blesser as long as Israel abides by the terms of the covenant. Israel's role in the relationship is not simply as a passive recipient of blessing: she is in actual danger, threatened by deception and idolatry (Deuteronomy 11:16), and must guard against her own tendencies to stray from the safety and full provision of the Lord.

The Israelites are literally asked to do no more, and no less, than listen to God's teaching and obey in trust. Why obey? "Do them, that you may live, and go in and take possession of the land that the LORD, the God of your fathers, is giving you," and "that will be your wisdom and your understanding" (Deuteronomy 4:1, 6).

Unmerited Blessing

Obedience did not—and does not—merit blessing. In addition to forty years of fallen wandering, Deuteronomy 7:7–8 explicitly states God's love was not founded upon the desirability of the people. It is only because she will be the object of God's favorable actions that Israel will be blessed:

> It was not because you were more in number than
> any other people that the LORD set His love on

> you and chose you, for you were the fewest of all peoples, but it is because the LORD loves you and is keeping the oath that He swore to your fathers, that the LORD has brought you out with a mighty hand and redeemed you from the house of slavery, from the hand of Pharaoh king of Egypt. (Deuteronomy 7:7–8)

In Deuteronomy 9:6, the Lord says, "Know, therefore, that the LORD your God is not giving you this good land to possess because of your righteousness, for you are a stubborn people." God's subsequent love lies in His desire to send His Son into the flesh and maintain His pledge of blessing to the patriarchs.

That does not mean that God will not repay those who hate Him. It is a personal thing to our Lord to be distrusted, disobeyed, and so rejected:

> Know therefore that the LORD your God is God, the faithful God who keeps covenant and steadfast love with those who love Him and keep His commandments, to a thousand generations, and repays to their face those who hate Him, by destroying them. (Deuteronomy 7:9–10a)

Still, the good news predominates. God wants to bless. He offers His favor, makes His expectations known, and grounds obedience in trust only after repeated acts of goodness, righteousness, and rescue. He warns them of their harmful tendencies and guides them toward safety and prosperity.

There are seven *baruk* formulas in the covenantal promises. In Deuteronomy 7:14, "You shall be blessed above all peoples," the context shows that *baruk* has the passive meaning, "someone who has experienced God's blessing." It also shows that the formulas are indicative statements referring to the future: "You *will be* more blessed than all other nations." These blessings are not mere wishes or abstractions. The Israelites will benefit from their entirely unearned relationship with their God, the God of Abraham, Isaac, and Jacob.[5]

Externals and Internals

Still, we must not assume that the obedience God requires is mechanical or external:

> And now, Israel, what does the LORD your God require of you, but to fear the LORD your God, to walk in all His ways, to love Him, to serve the LORD your God with all your heart and with all your soul. . . . Circumcise therefore the foreskin of your heart, and be no longer stubborn. (Deuteronomy 10:12, 16)

In this context, fear, walk, love, and serve pertain to the whole person. Stubbornness is a matter of the heart. Verse 16 reminds the people that circumcision was never about mere externals or a human act, but about the relationship between the Lord and His people. Circumcision could occur on the Sabbath, because it was a matter of God and not of man (John 7:21–23).

The obedience God seeks is actively against idolatry. It *practices* both trust in the Lord and love toward one's neighbor, precisely because these things are not always instinctive.

It comes down to a single, often misunderstood expression; what does it mean to *keep* God's commands? Does it mean to treasure and tend, as Adam was to keep his garden? to cherish as God keeps us? Or does it mean to obey by rote externals? How we answer affects how we understand the New Testament verse "Blessed rather are those who hear the word of God and keep it!" (Luke 11:28).

Our Lord grounded the covenant in Himself (Deuteronomy 10:17–22). He offers it explicitly out of love and for the sake of His promises to the patriarchs. He neither hides nor diminishes the truth of the Israelites' sin and rebellion, but He relates to them favorably with great patience toward them after repeatedly saving them in miraculous ways with His gracious, life-giving Word.

The God of Abraham goes so far as to say:

> My soul shall not abhor [or loathe] you. . . . If you spurn My statutes, and if your soul abhors My rules . . . yet for all that, when they are in the land of their

> enemies [the blessings lost], I will not spurn them, neither will I abhor them. (Leviticus 26:11, 15, 44)

Although God would react personally to covenantal infractions to the point of withholding benefits, God would always remember and uphold the Abrahamic Blessing (Leviticus 26:42).

In the next chapter, our Lord warns:

> Take care lest your heart be deceived, and you turn aside and serve other gods and worship them; then the anger of the LORD will be kindled against you, and He will shut up the heavens, so that there will be no rain, and the land will yield no fruit, and you will perish quickly off the good land that the LORD is giving you. (Deuteronomy 11:16–17)

God cannot look favorably on idolatry in any form. He does not look favorably on lies or deception, which belong to the devil. "Take care lest your heart be deceived" is directly linked with turning aside and serving other gods (v. 16).

Those with false faith may serve God externally in order to receive temporal benefits, but they cannot actually fulfill the covenant. They cannot bring blessing upon themselves, as though God could be manipulated. Again, obedience does not merit blessing; obeying the voice of the Lord, who has mercy, is an obedience of faith and not externals.

That is the obedience to maintain the proper covenant relationship with God. That holistic obedience by faith is the human side of the Mosaic, or Sinai, Covenant. When each side upholds its mutual responsibilities, the agreement stands.

This is a case, like forensic justification, where legal terminology can help clarify. Within the vassal covenant, God seeks to bless the people as long as He legally can! The covenantal legislation describes blessing as the normal state of affairs unless there is gross disobedience by the people as a whole, with degrees of resistance and punishment largely dependent on whether Israel would listen to their God (Leviticus 26:14–28).

> Because of Jesus' guilty verdict on the cross, God, in His mercy, judges us "not guilty." In another legal metaphor, God enters covenants (or contracts) with man. In them, God seeks to remain within the relationship rather than seek divorce or legal separation, despite the failures on our side.

God is not waiting for impending faithlessness. He is waiting for His Son to become incarnate and pay the debt of our sin. "The Lord is not slow to fulfill His promise as some count slowness, but is patient toward you, not wishing that any should perish, but that all should reach repentance" (2 Peter 3:9).

God takes action for His people. He acts to bless, providing and making them to thrive. He acts to sustain, carrying them through trials and war, death and wilderness. He acts to forgive and mercifully saves time and again when His people have wandered.

And still, in our Lord Jesus Christ, our God takes action. He enters the wilderness, not as a pillar of cloud by day or a pillar of fire by night, but as flesh-and-blood man. He considers the manna sent for so long and becomes our own Bread from heaven. He forgives us our sins to restore us to a right relationship with the Father, and He urges us toward faithfulness toward God and love toward one another.

To the Glory of God

Deuteronomy 28:1–14 lists blessings and realms of blessing. Deuteronomy 28:3 describes the realms in this way: "You will be blessed in the city, and you will be blessed in the field" (CM; cf. Genesis 39:5). The figure of speech—or merism—implies that the Israelites will experience God's blessing in all aspects of commerce and domestic life.

Deuteronomy 28:4 uses common Deuteronomic terms to describe human, plant, and animal offspring as *baruk*. This is another figure of speech. The emphasis is on the reception of good benefits by the Israelites: there will be numerous and healthy offspring and abundant good produce. Similarly, "Blessed shall be your basket and your kneading bowl" (v. 5) can be paraphrased "You will be blessed with a full basket and full kneading trough" (CM)—our modern ears do well to remember the Small Catechism's ancient table prayer: "Bless us and these Your gifts, which we receive from Your bountiful goodness,"[6] as it seeks blessing on our daily bread for the strengthening of our bodies and souls.

The final formula, in 28:6, like the first, contains a double blessing formula employing a merism: "You will be blessed when you come in and when you go out" (CM). This figure of speech includes almost everything: trips to the market, trips to the well, and even trips to bathe.

"As far as the east is from the west, so far does He remove our transgressions from us" (Psalm 103:12), even as our Lord gathers the redeemed from the east, west, north, and south (Psalm 107:2–3). The extent of God's blessing cannot be exaggerated. It emanates from Him. He *delights* in doing good and multiplying His creation! Twice in Deuteronomy, Moses addresses God delighting to prosper Israel: Deuteronomy 28:63; 30:9.

And, as Israel acquired fame and glory among the nations, other nations would fear and respect the Lord (Deuteronomy 26:19). Israel's prosperity and dominion would be reason for all the peoples of the earth to fear God as the one over all the earth (Deuteronomy 28:10).

The triune God guides us away from deceit and temptation toward God's full provision. He urges it for our sake that we may receive the undeserved blessings earned and won by Him. And by it, He spreads His Word so that all may know He is God and turn from the way of death.

CHAPTER 8

The Blessed

If we consider for a moment what it looked like to the Israelites to be the blessed of God walking into Canaan, it looked like opportunity, new neighbors, and a lot of war. In a very real way, it looked like life as usual. Those who saw them coming into their lands had a very different view of "the blessed."

We can all imagine a state of being blessed, though it may look very different from the Old Testament examples. The root *brk* implies a state of blessing; however, interpreting it to mean essentially "forever blessed" is not appropriate for most contexts in the Old Testament. Rather, people wish upon others that they may be in a state of blessing with the one true God Himself, who cannot help but be forever blessed.

Still, when people interact, there is a definite sense that the blessed are situated in a favored position. If the blessed are protected, then what of those who suffer without protection?

Human perception fails us here. We cannot help but recall that God's greatest victory over sin looked like defeat and included the Father forsaking the divine Son. Or, to cite common Old Testament themes, our God not only conquers but also delivers, protects, and rescues.

The answer is necessarily "Don't trust perception." As Martin Luther pointed out in discussing the theology of the cross, human ideas about glory quickly run contrary to God's revelation: "For the word of the cross is folly to those who are perishing, but to us who are being saved it is the power of God" (1 Corinthians 1:18).

Being blessed consists in being favored by God. Although we might be tempted to expect greater signs, that alone is an immeasurable expression of grace for the sake of Jesus Christ! Having said that, blessings also accompany us on our way, sustaining us as a gift of God, although they may be more reminiscent of Christ's cross than a life of ease.

God warns against thinking, "My own ability and strength brought me this prosperity" (Deuteronomy 8:17). Rather, from Genesis to Revelation, God shows us His unearned, forgiving favor, recording blessings that we might believe, rejoice, and give thanks to our saving Lord.

In some of His closing words, He blesses: "the one who keeps the words of the prophecy of [Revelation]" and "those who wash their robes [in the blood of the Lamb], so that they may have the right to the tree of life and that they may enter the city by the gates" (Revelation 22:14). Here we see blessing tied to the Word, which God sends out, as well as to Baptism and salvation. The Word of God was central to the Mosaic Covenant, and it is central to Christ's Covenant.

With these holy gifts, God establishes His favorable presence with us. By them, our own flesh and blood can experience His love. So until the golden age of the New Jerusalem comes, we have the priceless print of the Word of God and His eternal gifts of salvation and forgiveness to sustain us until Christ comes again.

In the meantime, however, we can gain insight explicitly into how others viewed the blessed status of the Israelites through the narratives about Balaam. We can see the desires of Canaanites, who would not willingly relinquish their land to the God of Abraham.

Divination and Balaam

The narratives of Balaam may be particularly suited to testify to the steadfast nature of God's blessing, even in appearing to an unbelieving diviner. It was unknown until later that Balaam spoke divination blessings to their benefit.

Divination is employed to determine the will of God regarding the person(s) to be blessed. If divination reveals that God is not favorably disposed, or is angry at the person(s), then a curse predicting downfall may be uttered in place of a blessing. A striking feature of this type of blessing is that it does not presuppose that the blesser believes in Yahweh, or even in a single god. The method of divination employed is quite similar to that used in extrabiblical ancient Near Eastern religions.

Laban used divination to determine that it was because of Jacob that Yahweh had blessed him (Genesis 30:27). However, Laban did not utter a blessing pronouncement; he simply conceded to Jacob that Jacob had been the mediator of God's blessing.

Divination blessing pronouncements are declarations that describe the relationship between God and the person(s) blessed. They declare that God is favorably disposed toward certain persons and that God therefore has blessed them and/or will bless them in the future.

The only true divination pronouncements are in the Balaam narratives. Both in the Balaam narratives and in later references to them, the Piel of *brk* is declarative, meaning "to declare that someone has been and will continue to be a recipient of blessings from their God." The Piel occurs in Numbers 22:6; 23:11 twice; 20 twice, 25 twice; 24:1, 10 twice; Joshua 24:10 twice. The noun *berakah* occurs in Deuteronomy 23:6 and Nehemiah 13:2 denoting the four pronouncements Balaam uttered in Numbers 22–24. The Pual is found in Numbers 22:6, meaning "to receive benefits from God."[1]

Archaeology has shed much light on the Balaam narrative. Balaam is no longer a mysterious character. There is now a great deal of material available illustrating the practice of divination and various related sorts of prophecy in the ancient Near East. Balaam closely resembles a *baru,* a type of diviner who was quite common, especially in Mesopotamia.

There is good evidence that the Mesopotamian practices of divination were also common in Canaan in the second millennium. In times of war, diviners helped develop battle strategy. Sometimes a diviner even led an army into battle.

The *baru* had several methods of divination that he frequently used. One of the most common was examination of the remains of sacrificed animals. Extispicy inspected entrails, and hepatoscopy attempted to read livers.

Balaam was hired by Balak because of the threat of war with Israel

(Numbers 22:1–6). He proceeded to build seven altars on three separate occasions and make sacrifices in order to obtain a divine oracle (Numbers 23:1–5, 14–17, 29–30; cf. 22:40; 24:1). In short, he acted like a typical *baru.*

Balaam seeks his oracles from Yahweh. This also is perfectly in keeping with his role. Since Yahweh is Israel's God, Balaam must find out Israel's fate from Yahweh. It would do no good to consult Baal or Ishtar about a people that lie outside of their jurisdiction. The references to Yahweh do not make Balaam a monotheist or a worshiper of Yahweh—when inquiring about another people, Balaam would consult their god.

(Imagine believing one's god was bound to mountains or the sea! Imagine consulting oracles to see whether one's god were willing to travel into battle in order to expand his limited territory! The God of creation is largely unique in His claim to be God of land and sea, heaven and earth.)

Balaam had a reputation as an effective diviner. His widespread fame is now illustrated by an Aramaic text dating from about 700 BC from Deir 'Alla.[2] The picture of Balaam in this text agrees with the biblical description of him as a professional diviner (Joshua 13:22). Based on divination, Balaam, as a professional, declares people to be headed either toward fortune or misfortune.

There is no agent stated for the passive verbs, implying that the agents are the gods (as in other biblical impersonal constructions with God implied as the agent). There is no question, then, about the manner in which Balaam's benedictions or maledictions take effect. In this biblical narrative, it is clear that Balaam does *not* have an exceptional ability to pronounce powerful formulas that effect what they state. Neither are the words prayers or wishes for God to bless/curse. Rather, Balaam is a diviner. His skill lies in his ability to *predict* the future based on the examination of signs, not in making events occur.

Balak summoned Balaam to curse Israel. He said, "Now, come and curse this people for me because they are stronger than I. Perhaps I will be able to defeat them and drive them from the land, for I know that whomever you bless gets blessed, and whomever you curse gets cursed" (Numbers 22:6 CM).

Balak states that those whom Balaam pronounces blessed/cursed actually meet the fate he predicts. *Meborak* and *yu'ar* do not merely describe the people as having formulas spoken over them, but emphasize the actual reception of fortune/misfortune.

In Numbers 22, Balaam asks God if he should comply; he receives a nocturnal answer in verse 12: "Do not curse the people, because they are blessed" (CM). Some scholars, such as Brichto and Wehmeier, understand *baruk* as meaning "immune to a spell"; however, if Israel were immune to curses, there would be no need for God to prevent Balaam from cursing her.

God's preventative measures indicate that perhaps Balaam's curse would indeed have had deleterious effects. Yahweh prevented Balaam from cursing Israel because such a curse would have prophesied the disfavor and anger of Yahweh upon His people and their consequent defeat in battle.

Such a curse would have inaccurately represented the relationship between Yahweh and Israel, and since it is important for Yahweh that others correctly perceive this relationship, He changes the curses into declarations of His favor toward Israel.

Yahweh prevents Balaam from cursing. He tells Balaam that Israel is *baruk* (22:12). "Blessed" means that Israel stands in a favorable relationship to God; God had blessed and would continue to bless her out of His favor for her. God's favor toward Israel is made clear by His blesser/blessed relationship with her. Balaam cannot predict that God will abandon or be angry with His people and so let them be defeated.

Balaam then asks . . . (Numbers 23:8, 20 CM):

> How can I curse (*qbb*) him whom God has not cursed?
> How can I curse (*z'm*) him whom Yahweh has not cursed?
> See, I have received a command to bless;
> He has blessed, and I cannot change it.

Balaam's frequent assertion that he can speak only what Yahweh tells him (22:8, 18, 35, 38; 23:3–5, 12, 16, 26; 24:13) is perfectly consistent with his role. He cannot simply say what he is paid to say. When he finds out from the gods what will happen, he cannot change it; he can only relay the information to Balak (23:8, 20). Balaam is essentially a prophet, i.e., a spokesman for God. Here his main function is as predictor.

Balaam the prophet must accurately relay what God has told him. After the first two benedictions, Balaam stopped using divination: "When Balaam saw that it was pleasing to Yahweh to bless Israel, he did not employ divination as he had previously" (24:1 CM). Balaam felt that the previous oracles he had received clearly conveyed God's intentions, so that there was no longer any need for divination.

The benedictions spoken by Balaam contain descriptions of typical blessing benefits: fertility (23:10; 24:7), dominion (23:24; 24:8–9, 17–19; cf. 24:20–24), prosperity (24:5–7), and royalty (24:7, 17). Yahweh is with her (*'im,* 23:21) and has delivered her from Egypt (23:22; 24:8). The benedictions describe Israel as having been blessed in the past and destined for future blessing.

The strongest element is dominion—Israel will eat other nations as a lion devours its prey (23:24; 24:8–9) and will conquer Edom (24:18). The phrase "those on good terms with you will be blessed, while those hostile to you will be cursed" (CM) in 24:9 was apparently a standard formula expressing dominion (cf. Genesis 12:3; 26:29).

Israel's deliverance from Egypt and future dominion are emphasized because of the impending battles of the conquest. God's Word was going before His people to prepare the way. While peoples were preparing for war, God was speaking His blessing. His blessing, however, would not come apart from His promised woman's Seed, the offspring of Abraham.

In many ways, the conquest of Canaan is unique as a series of events. God is careful to reveal His will publicly. He makes widely known that the victories are His own. Yet His own people must rely on His promises and trust His Word, while Balaam and his donkey see the angel of the Lord (Numbers 22:22–30).

Special Blessings upon the King

As Israel becomes a nation, and after the people have demanded a king, God reveals a special blessing for the king of Israel as His vice-regent (Psalms 21:1–7; 45:3; cf. 1 Kings 2:45). The king mediates blessing to the people (see Psalm 72:17). God aids the king in battle, in administrative and judicial duties, and in other enterprises in order to preserve the welfare of the people.

Would a "blessed king" meet more of our expectations for fame and renown? Perhaps. People expected God specially to bless the king. It also falls under the Patriarchal Promise of royal descendants (Genesis 17:16, 20; 35:9). However, if usurpation occurred—or if military defeat, famine, or poverty characterized his reign—there was no guarantee of job security. The people could simply conclude that God had withdrawn his *ḥesed,* the "grace of kingship," from the king, as God did from Saul (2 Samuel 7:15) .

God's promise to David of a lasting dynasty in 2 Samuel 7 and 1 Chronicles 17 is the most important promise regarding kingship. "The LORD swore to David a sure oath from which He will not turn back: 'One of the sons of your body I will set on your throne' " (Psalm 132:11).

Although the Israelites prayed for grace upon their ruler—as should we all—thanks be to God that it is Christ, our Lord, who ultimately and eternally fulfills this blessing. So that, though we long for earthly rulers of strength and integrity, Jesus remains on His throne.

This blessing was not the simple expression of nationalism it initially appears to be. Yes, it affirms Israel as God's chosen people, with God active in minutiae, but it, too, relates back to God's original purpose of blessing all nations by sending His Son into the world.

Special Blessings upon Zion

A blessed people, a blessed person, and then a blessed land come to our attention. Three passages in the Psalms discuss how God looks with particular fondness upon Zion, the great hill of Jerusalem, and so has made it, or her, the special object of His blessing.[3]

Zion is a source of blessing for the nation because God's blessings upon her spread to the borders of the nation, and for her sake God preserves the entire nation. These statements are fulfillments of God's promises in Exodus 20:24; Psalm 132:13–15. The Creator's concern for creation becomes tied with the place of His activity, the site of His temple, and the city of His people.

Psalm 147 calls for Jerusalem to praise God for restoring her in the second temple period:

For He strengthens the bars of your gates;
  He blesses your children within you.
He makes peace in your borders;
He fills you with the finest of the wheat. (Psalm 147:13–14)

The inhabitants are described affectionately as children, and *berak* refers to their ability to live a good life, presumably by bestowing such things as children, food, health, and peace. Zion is a place for prosperity and safety.

Psalm 133 is a short psalm of ascent describing the beauty of "brothers sitting together" in corporate worship:

Behold, how good and pleasant it is
  when brothers dwell in unity!
It is like the precious oil on the head,
  running down on the beard,
on the beard of Aaron,
  running down on the collar of his robes!
It is like the dew of Hermon,
  which falls on the mountains of Zion!
For there the LORD has commanded the blessing,
life forevermore. (Psalm 133)

This stresses that God's election of Zion has made Zion a source of blessing for the nation. Zion is God's resting place, and so it is the place from which He blesses (Psalms 128:5; 134:3; 1 Kings 8).

God has stationed His blessing on Mount Zion, and from there it spreads to the people. Blessing is only indirectly linked to dew; the thought of dew leads the psalmist to mention blessing.[4]

Psalm 84 also associates blessing with Zion, alluding to those making a pilgrimage:

> As they go through the Valley of Baca
>   they make it a place of springs;
>   the early rain also covers it with pools.
> They go from strength to strength;
> each one appears before God in Zion. (Psalm 84:6–7)

The motif of water in the desert is characteristic of the prophetic apocalypses. Here, the psalmist describes how the arid desert seems like a verdant valley to the pilgrims because of their joyful anticipation of entering the temple courts.

Prophetic Apocalyptic Blessing Promises

The ultimate state of blessedness for Christians will be heaven and the re-creation with the second coming of Christ. The Old Testament prophesies it, describing it beautifully in terms of a golden age of blessing. In these Apocalyptic Blessing Promises, prophets address the nation as a whole regarding blessings not experienced within the hearers' lifetime.

The prophets describe the coming eternal salvation as the inauguration of a state of blessing. Is blessing given once, granting all immunity? Of course not. Rather, God deals more intimately than that. Within a state of blessing, God is continually giving in favor, and we are continually receiving.

Those in a state of blessing still perpetually need God.

God promises to inaugurate the age of blessing through acts of deliverance (Ezekiel 34:22; cf. Isaiah 19:20; 61:9; 65:23; Ezekiel 34:10, 12, 27). In Isaiah 51:1–3; 65:17–25, God effects blessing by performing a second creation; the blessed state is part of "new heavens and a new earth" and a new Jerusalem (65:17–18). In Isaiah 44:3, God promotes the state of blessing by pouring out His Spirit.

The blessings often consist of fertility or prosperity, but the thought soon turns from these ordinary benefits to extraordinary and even miraculous benefits. In these passages, God does not quietly effect blessing: He dramatically intervenes in the course of history. God promises to deliver His people and inaugurate a golden age of blessing through His acts of deliverance. In Isaiah 65:17–25, God clearly blesses through a second creation.

Now that Christ is risen and the New Testament is ours to proclaim, we can recognize just how dramatically God did intervene, albeit through a relatively quiet pregnancy and birth followed by growth and adolescence, Jesus' early ministry, and His victory over death. And there is more to come with the sound of trumpets and Christ's triumphant return! His new creations by faith will enter into the new Jerusalem and paradise.

Much like Jesus speaking His parables, the prophets' Apocalyptic Blessings often address the physical benefits the people likely desired. Those benefits, however, are of secondary importance to the other benefits God promises. The material blessings promised are often only symbols of more abstract benefits, such as God's favor and peace.

In Ezekiel 34:26, God promises, "I will make them and the areas around My hill recipients of blessing. I will make rain come down in its season; they will be rains giving blessing" (CM). The context clearly describes the nation as receiving blessing. Conversely, the second phrase does not denote rains that have received blessing, but rains that bring God's blessing to the nations. God's blessing here consists of agricultural fertility (v. 27), as often in apocalyptic prophecies (for example, Hosea 2:22; Joel 3:18; Amos 9:13–14; Zechariah 8:12), but fertility shrinks in importance next to the other benefits God promises.

God will raise up a David figure as leader over the nations (Ezekiel 34:23–24). He will banish predators from the land (v. 25). God will make a covenant giving peace with them (v. 25). And let us note that peace, *shalom,* is not some sort of negation, as though peace is simply a time without trouble or worry. It is a thoroughly positive concept speaking of a state in which everything is going, and functioning, well.

In Christ, God provides a Sower and Shepherd to cast the seed of His Word and gather the sheep of His making. In Christ, He has a perfect divine King for the human throne of Israel and the Mediator of the new covenant, "so that those who are called may receive the promised eternal inheritance, since a death has occurred that redeems them from the transgressions committed under the first covenant" (Hebrews 9:15).

In Christ, we are new creations, crafted by the Father's loving hand. Isaiah 65:17–25 is a passage that describes the future golden age as a new creation. God promises that the people will be a "generation blessed by Yahweh" (65:23; similarly, Isaiah 61:9). This passage is often used to describe life after the resurrection, although some of the blessing benefits are not interpreted literally.

In the context, God's blessing consists of fertility, longevity, prosperity, and peace. Yet these benefits are more spectacular than they are in the other types of promises. People will normally live to over one hundred years (Isaiah 65:20), and it will be assumed that anyone who dies at less than one hundred has incurred God's disfavor (cf. Genesis 38:7, 10)!

That is not to imply that those who die before age 100 now have died in God's judgment. Rather, consider common causes of death at that time: disease, malnutrition, and war. These are put at a distance by God's will for His people.

After the resurrection of Christ, we see the full extent of God's distancing His people from death. We will rise like Jesus, changed and imperishable, in bodies like His (1 Corinthians 15:51–53). Not only is God creating the world anew, but creation is tied with deliverance, salvation, sanctification, and righteousness in a perfect state of perpetual blessedness!

Isaiah 51:1–3 is concerned with demonstrating how God faithfully fulfills even His most unbelievable promise. God uses Abraham as an example of such a fulfillment:

> Listen to Me, you who pursue righteousness,
>   you who seek the LORD:
> look to the rock from which you were hewn,
>   and to the quarry from which you were dug.
> Look to Abraham your father
>   and to Sarah who bore you;

for he was but one when I called him,
that I might bless him and multiply him.
For the Lord comforts Zion;
He comforts all her waste places
and makes her wilderness like Eden,
her desert like the garden of the Lord;
joy and gladness will be found in her,
thanksgiving and the voice of song. (Isaiah 51:1–3)

The comparison of Abraham to a rock describes the origin of the nation as an act of creation. A rock is barren and inanimate, incapable of producing anything by itself. It was only because God fulfilled His blessing promise that Abraham fathered Isaac, leading to the emergence of the nation. Though the nation lies in ruins (Isaiah 51:3), Israel is encouraged to trust that just as God made one man into a multitude, so He will again rebuild the nation. The rebuilt nation in verse 3 is pictured as a second creation, another Eden, full of joy and praise.

In the hands of the Word by whom all things were made, however, Jesus uses a rock metaphor to describe His Word (Matthew 7:24–25) and Peter's confession (Matthew 16:18). God is building a foundation of the prophets and apostles by His Word (Ephesians 2:19–21), and from the Rock that is Christ all drink the same spiritual drink by the provision of Christ (1 Corinthians 10:1–4).

Parts of the Prophetic Apocalyptic Blessing Promises directly incorporate other peoples into Israel. In Isaiah 61:5, foreigners are incorporated into Israel, rather like the Gibeonites, to serve her. Although they are not given equal status with Israel, they remain unconquered. In Jeremiah 4:2 and Isaiah 19:24–25, other nations partake of the blessings given Israel. Jeremiah 4:1–2 also alludes to the Patriarchal Promises. If the people return to God and serve Him faithfully, then "all nations will acquire blessing through [the Lord], and will exult in Him" (CM)[5]

Most passages, however, are concerned solely with the internal condition of Israel and her relationship to God. Isaiah 44:3 describes how God's blessing will renew religious commitment among the Israelites:

For I will pour water on the thirsty land,
    and streams on the dry ground;
I will pour My Spirit upon your offspring,
and My blessing on your descendants.

The figure of plant fertility is used here. God's blessing activity will be like pouring water on dry ground, enabling plants to grow (v. 4), but the prophet is not primarily concerned with fertility. The effect of God's blessing is described in verse 5:

This one will say, "I am the LORD's,"
    another will call on the name of Jacob,
and another will write on his hand, "The LORD's,"
and name himself by the name of Israel.

Note God's beneficent influence on the religion of the people: the effect of God's blessing and Spirit being poured out is that the people will return to the traditional faith and declare their loyalty to Yahweh (v. 5). They will proudly take the names of the patriarchs to symbolize their adherence to the ancient, God-given faith. The people will want the undeserved mercy and blessing of the Abrahamic and Patriarchal Promises. Clinging to God's forgiving history, they realign themselves with the fathers of the faith.

And if Israel repents, other nations would see the benefits Israel would then derive from her covenant relationship to God. The other nations would seek to enter that relationship in order to acquire blessing from Yahweh too. Jeremiah predicts the inclusion of all the nations in the worship of Yahweh also in Jeremiah 3:17 (on jealousy as a means of conversion, cf. Deuteronomy 32:21b; Romans 10:19; 11:11b).

CHAPTER 9

Human Blessings

We have seen a father blessing his sons and a leader blessing his people. These blessings were initiated by God Himself, but man also had a role in them. God remains the ultimate giver of every good gift, but man can be authorized to share what God has given him.

Human blessings, like God's blessings, can consist of a speech act or a bestowal of material goods. Both types display the favor and goodwill of the blesser. Some blessings also describe the relationship between God and the person blessed.

This category of blessings in particular reflects our own widespread usage. While there is a tendency today to say something is a blessing because it is basically good, the Scriptures are clear that all blessings actually belong to God alone, though it pleases Him to share them through others. Blessings are neither generic nor automatic: they may be given only according to the Word of God. Yet ours is a God who even wishes enemies and persecutors to turn toward Him and receive blessing (Luke 6:27–28; Romans 12:14; 1 Peter 3:9).

Some Old Testament blessings are spoken in the temple or court, but most are spoken in everyday life situations. Sometimes there is a favorable relationship between God and the person blessed and other times not. Many are simple greetings and farewells, well-wishes, or an expression of appreciation or astonishment.

Expectations of the participants vary. Mere wishes may go unfulfilled, while warmth effectively carries through. In Scripture, depending on the person, speaking blessings can attain the level of a formal religious declaration or prediction.

Human blessings are capable of expressing warmth, appreciation, goodwill, and a variety of other sentiments, while typically fulfilling societal roles. As a social custom, blessings generally gravitate more toward letting the recipient feel appreciated rather than actually acquiring additional benefits to the person blessed.

In addition to the human power of words, there are three reasons to consider why God may add His power toward fulfillment: (1) God is often invoked in the formula to bless, and He listens to those who invoke His name; (2) the blessings rely on God's general retribution—God generally wants the hungry fed, and so on; and (3) the blessings rely on God's responsiveness to prayer. The extent of results, then, lies primarily in the Lord's hands.

Social Situations

Blessing are typical greetings around the world. Sayings such as *Vaya con Dios* ("Go with God"), *Adios* ("to God"), and *Adieu* ("to God") are words of blessing directly linked with religion. Other expressions, such as *Gesundheit,* wish good health without an explicit mention of God.

Such blessings are so common they have become a cultural expression. People may no longer even realize what they are saying. For example, how many of us look for a meaning or definition behind "hello" and "hi"? In a sense, there is none other than serving the purpose of getting one's attention. Good-bye, on the other hand, is a grammatical contraction of "God be with you/ye." *Farewell* is also a blessing, wishing that the one departing may fare well.

In our society, many hear "Bless you" and presume the triune God as the beneficial one who blesses, and that is essentially true. All good things come from the triune God (James 1:17), yet blessings are not solely sought, given, or discussed within Christianity.

There are rites, rituals, formulas, and expressions in Hinduism, for example, with no direct connection to the Old or New Testaments. This demonstrates that many bless in the name of a different god. Not all blessings heard by the human ear are Christian blessings.

In Scripture, the Piel of *brk* can be used with the simple meaning "to greet" or "to say good-bye." They are benedictions in the sense that they "speak good to" someone. Although "benediction" can carry a particular liturgical association, human blessings are spoken formulas that call upon God to bless another person.

Occasionally these greetings are recorded as having the same form as a formal prayer, but they do not request specific benefits from God. Instead, they use general expressions such as "May God be with you" or "May God bless you" (see Ruth 2:4).

Those who uttered such expressions in Scripture, like so often today, normally do not expect them to be fulfilled in a striking manner. The greetings and farewells are social customs that usually have little religious value. They are illocutionary utterances whose main importance is the perlocutionary effect: expressing goodwill, friendship, affection, and occasionally, religious fellowship.

Because of their social function, *brk* is sometimes simply translated "to greet" or "to say farewell," rather than "to bless," unless there seems to be a specific religious function or a direct invocation of God.

The greetings and farewells could be uttered in a variety of situations. They could be spoken by those in authority, by subordinates to those over them, and between equals. Ruth 2:4; 2 Kings 4:29; and Proverbs 27:14 indicate that they were commonly used in everyday life, probably more frequently than on formal occasions such as in Genesis 47:7, 10.

And, just as we sometimes do today, when we say, greet so-and-so for me, different words may actually constitute the salutation. It is difficult to generalize about the content of Scripture greetings and farewells, because they are infrequently recorded. Naturally they would be shaped by the situation: a simple *shalom* (peace) would probably suffice for meeting a stranger on the road. Among strangers or those of different religious persuasions, a deity might not be invoked (none is in 1 Samuel 25:5–6), but the pious, and those wishing to appear pious, invoked Yahweh (Ruth 2:4; 1 Samuel 15:13).

It is evident that not everyone uses religious blessings honestly. After Saul defeated the Amalekites, "Samuel came to Saul, and Saul said to him, 'May you be blessed by Yahweh. I have fulfilled Yahweh's word' " (1 Samuel 15:13 CM). The formula is a general salutary benediction. Saul is not praying for any specific benefit for Samuel, but is simply wishing him well.

Saul used that greeting because he wished to appear pious. He had *not* in fact obeyed God's command to exterminate the Amalekites completely. Here, and in 1 Samuel 13:10, where Saul offered the sacrifice before Samuel arrived, Saul probably felt guilty because of his disobedience and sought to forestall Samuel's anger by greeting him piously. Saul's words of greeting are not recorded in 13:10, but they probably were similar to the salutation of 15:13.

Proverbs 27:14 says that the social custom of greeting must be performed in the socially accepted manner and context in order for it to have the desired perlocutionary forces. Although that could sound formal to some, we might agree that shouting hello first thing in the morning is typically not the way to wish someone well!

Most greetings and farewells, and many of the thanksgiving and praise benedictions, are primarily expressions of the speaker's sentiments. The speaker rarely expects these benedictions to be fulfilled literally. The benedictions imply little or nothing about the relationship between God and the addressee, who may be a perfect stranger (see, for example, Genesis 47:7, 10; 1 Samuel 25:14; 2 Kings 4:29). They do express the fact that the speaker is favorably disposed toward the addressee.

The Old Testament records enough accounts that we know that blessing greetings and conversations were common while traveling, even between strangers (2 Kings 4:29). Jacob went so far as to speak greeting and farewell benedictions to Pharaoh, a pagan king, in thanks and respect (Genesis 47:7, 10). Blessing greetings were used as deference to a sovereign (cf. Ruth 2:4b; 1 Kings 8:66).

At the same time, greetings are not always secular in nature. In 2 Kings 10:15, Jehu greets Jehonadab with a view toward establishing a common religious bond. Jehu has been killing Baal worshipers. When Jehonadab affirms that he is of a similar mind with Jehu, Jehu takes him into his chariot and continues his pursuit (vv. 16–17).

Also, Ruth 2:4 quotes two greeting benedictions: "Just then Boaz came from Bethlehem. He said to the reapers, 'May Yahweh be with you!' They said to him, 'May Yahweh bless you!' " (CM). This exchange describes greetings in everyday life among the pious. The reapers respond to Boaz's piety by also invoking Yahweh. Boaz's call for God's presence is no less forceful than the reapers' response using the jussive Piel of *brk*. There is no indication that Boaz's words constitute a wish for a plentiful harvest. Both expressions are more salutations than prayers. The salutations imply that the two parties are on friendly terms and share a common religious bond.

In Scripture, *brk* serves as a greeting that

- lays groundwork toward a positive relationship;
- may or may not invoke God;
- may serve simply as a hello or farewell;
- may express a common religious bond; and
- may pray for the other's well-being.

Culture

Such blessing greetings can also remind us that, though there can be cultural uses of religious language, a proper understanding can slip away. Words have power, but their usage can also slip into a man-centered exchange.

A time may come when people remember that *holiday* comes from *holy day*, and that *good-bye* was also originally a religious term. Such simple, carefree expressions may cause a reaction, although it is often hard to predict when cultural scenarios will play out with dramatic flair.

Still, even the smallest Christian gestures can be bold, though it may be unintentional on our part. We can pray that those who part from us will indeed fare well, and we can do that in the words we already use. We can remember God's abundant goodness when "bless you" slips out as a reflex, because God surely does bless, particularly through sending His Son to be the Savior of the world.

As cultures and societies change, it is good to remember that blessings are not, and never have been, a universal concept. But, as the religious nature slips—or is stripped—away, Christians do not need to miss the key aspects to just how rich blessings are.

Christians cannot presume that because words are common, everyone must know what they mean. Sadly, some people think Easter is Jesus' birthday. Cultural inclusion of religious words can bear a negative effect on both the cultured and the churched. The cultured remain mired in their assumptions, often presuming God's favor yet excluding God, and the churched can forget the depths of God's terminology and the many temptations within human understanding.

As cultures shift, we may no longer take for granted any sort of culturally favored status for the faith. Our words and ways may need a closer look as we reexamine ourselves in light of changing times. That, too, is likely a gift from our gracious God.

It is perhaps ironic that there are explicitly religious phrases that enter nonreligious vocabularies. "Thank God," for example, has become proverbial, something inherited from culture and common language. It may not express a confession in the belief of any god whatsoever, yet it can remind us of the many ways, and the many-leveled approach, God uses in blessing us, from sending rain to growing crops to giving us every form of daily—and heavenly—bread.

But what of unbelievers who bless when they raise a glass and say, "Salute!/Salud" ("to your health"), "Prost!" ("to your advantage"), and other variants wishing long life, cheer, honor ("to you!")? What are the connections between well-wishing and blessing, by Christians or otherwise? Who exactly can bless?

Well-Wishing

People make wishes all the time. In linguistic terms, wishes are expressed by the optative mood—speaking of what you would opt or choose. Sometimes, we use helpful expressions to show we are making a wish, including such words and phrases as "if only," "could," "would," or "may," while other times it is just implied.

Not every wish is well-wishing. Well-wishing is an expression of goodwill from one person to another, and it is not unusual for some benefit to be included within that hope. One can see an immediate parallel with blessing, and blessings can certainly be made in optative form.

The majority of human blessings are optative. Optative blessings are always wishes or prayers for God to bless. The optative blessings are an expression of the speaker's sentiments. They may be spoken out of thanks or praise to a benefactor, as a greeting or farewell to express friendship or fellowship, or as a prayer for someone the speaker cares about. They, too, never have a magical or self-fulfilling power, although they can influence God and cause Him to bless.

The importance of the identity of the speaker in performative utterances has obvious implications for blessing. The effectiveness of God's promise and benedictions is based on His ability to bestow fertility, wealth, dominion, health, and other benefits. The Covenantal Blessings outlined by Moses are likewise effective because Moses is God's spokesman, and when the people pronounce the blessings in the covenant renewal ceremony (Joshua 8:33–34), the people are speaking according to God's instructions through Moses.

The Priestly Blessing, discussed in chapter 11, is effective because the priests mediate on behalf of God. God promises to honor their benedictions (Numbers 6:27). God strikingly fulfilled Eli the priest's blessing of Hannah (1 Samuel 2:20–21). When the kings bless the people, they, like the priests, have an effective blessing because of their status as mediators.

Yet other blessings can be spoken by anyone, not just specially authorized persons. Many of the greetings, thanksgivings, praises, and wishes are spoken by ordinary people in everyday situations.

Blessings, and blessing formulas, express God's approval. Sometimes, the expressions are God's words given to a prophet. Other times, God simply works through man's own words.

It must be said, however, that in Scripture these blessings are much less effective than those spoken by God or by God's representatives. They are purely social customs that society—and the speaker—do not expect to be fulfilled immediately or in a dramatic manner.

Outside of select roles, people speak blessings to one another largely as well-wishes. They are illocutionary utterances, and the speech conveys the speaker's goodwill. The fact that they are optative wishes means that the speaker is at least partially uncertain whether or not his utterance will be fulfilled.

There is a custom in which a man seeks a blessing from his potential father-in-law before proposing to his potential bride. The custom can demonstrate respect for one's elders, in mind of the Fourth Commandment, and the reality that marriage joins two families as well as two individuals. Perhaps it used to fill a more legal function as well. Father is certainly a select role with both practical and religious implications, yet it appears to be more of a cultural use of the expression "blessing" than a religiously revealed one.

Baruk used in human optative benedictions calls for *God* to bless the person, not simply for the person to possess benefits. God is pictured as the ultimate source of blessing throughout the Bible because blessing is a result of a favorable relationship to God.

When a person blesses, it is not because blessing is a power given by God (or another) that a person can control, determine, and distribute as he wishes. The ability to bless is not something man can possess apart from God. All the types of optative blessings explicitly or implicitly call on God to fulfill them when a fulfillment is expected.

> Well-wishing expresses a person's favor.
> Blessing calls upon God to express His favor.
> The two can certainly overlap.

Vocation

"Blessing" can be a noun or a verb. We have spoken at length about blessing as a declaration, as a verb of speech. We addressed physical benefits commonly understood to be blessings as a noun. People can be blessings too: "[Abram] will be a blessing" (Genesis 12:2).

The root *brk* is used only a few times to denote human good deeds (or *benefaction*). The Piel means "to treat with respect, treat well, be on good terms with" and as a noun can mean either "benefaction" (good deed) or gift. Still, this does not mean that blessing loses its inherent connection with God's favor. In Genesis 12:2, God declares that

Abram "will be a blessing." God's favor, in big things and little things, can—and is—mediated.

As John Kleinig notes:

> In keeping with God's law those who have received God's blessing can pass it on by blessing others. Parents may bless their children (Gen. 27:28–29, 39; 48:15–16). Leaders in a community may bless a couple at their wedding (Gen. 21:60; Ruth 4:11–12). Kings may bless their people (Gen. 14:18–20; 2 Sam. 6:18; 1 Kings 8:55–61). People may greet another people with a blessing on meeting them (Gen. 47:7; Ruth 2:4; 1 Sam. 13:10; 15:13; 2 Kings 4:29) or leaving them (Gen. 24:60; 28:3–4; 31:55; 47:10; 2 Sam. 19:39).
>
> Second, in the order of redemption, God authorizes his priests to bless His people in His name.[1]

Solomon's blessing prayer in 1 Kings 8:15–53 describes the temple as having an important function for mediating blessing to the nation. The temple makes God and His grace accessible. Previously, God had not designated any of the places where He had made His presence known as *the* place where His name resided (v. 16). Now, people could pray toward the temple in Jerusalem and rest assured that God would respond to their prayer.

Although God was not confined to the temple (v. 27; vv. 30, 32, 34, 36, 43, 49 picture God in heaven), the temple was the visible sign of God's presence. God is pictured as responding to prayers for blessings that are directed toward the temple. God bestows rain and delivers His people from famine, sickness, locusts, national enemies, and exile (vv. 33–34, 36–37, 47–49). All these benefits are part of the Covenantal Blessing Promises.

God will even respond to the prayers of foreigners so that they fear Yahweh just as Israel does (vv. 42–43, 60). Through the temple, blessing can be mediated to all nations. In the second temple period, the temple continued to be a source of blessing for the people (see Haggai

2:19; Zechariah 8:13; Malachi 3:10; cf. Zion as a source of blessing, Psalms 128:5; 134:3; and the ark as a source of blessing, 2 Samuel 6:11–12 = 1 Chronicles 13:14). But how did God give such a gift?

Exodus 35 describes examples of vocation in the Old Testament. Men and women shared what they had in services and contributions, and God used it to His glory. Exodus 35:30–31 goes so far as to say that the Lord "has called by name" Bezalel and also

> has filled him with the Spirit of God, with skill, with intelligence, with knowledge, and with all craftsmanship, to devise artistic designs, to work in gold and silver and bronze, in cutting stones for setting, and in carving wood, for work in every skilled craft. (Exodus 35:31–33)

Carpentry and even such artisans of luxuries as gold workers and gem cutters are used by God to show His favor to His faithful. Vocation corresponds to blessing because they are ordered within creation to spread God's blessing to one's neighbor.

After all, God made marriage with a *husband* and *wife*. In parenthood, God blesses with *a child*. Prosperity can include additional workers. Inheritance is dependent upon parents, government with God-given authority, and so on. It is significant that Jacob attributes his ability to offer gifts to Esau to the fact that God had bestowed upon him the goods he wanted to give (Genesis 33:1–11). What makes vocation remarkable is not what we do, which may be done by nature or with poor intent, but that God can use our relationships and stations for the good and blessing of others!

As early as Genesis 4:21, Scripture records instrumentalists. During the reign of the blessed King David, he organized priests, but also musicians, gatekeepers, treasurers, and more. Different services functioned separately, but they came together in the service of the nation and God's promise to bless through that nation. The priesthood served those with sacrifices, and the priesthood of all believers offered their blessed sacrifices of thanks and praise to God in faith toward Him and love toward one another.

As of old, when God's presence was tied to Israel in the blesser/blessed relationship, we approach those outside the faith, bringing God along with us—not because of what we do, but because God has attached Himself to us in His mercy.

Blessings flow from the God of heaven and earth, preserving and maintaining creation. He gives new life to natural processes and gives according to need, sending rain on the just and the unjust according to His plentiful mercy (Matthew 5:45).

Deuteronomy 28:12 illustrates the way in which God actually would bestow His blessing: "Yahweh will open up His storehouse of good things, the heavens, to bestow rain upon your land in its season and bless all that you do with your hands" (CM).

Notice how God's action to bless is interwoven with natural processes. How does water come? Through rain. God can personally work through natural processes and, when blessing, He typically makes them work better than normal.

Some might consider working through such natural means impersonal, but is that really the case when one speaks of Him who created those natural processes? God places man as His representative over creation and shares His own love through men, women, and children of all ages. The Father sent His Son into our very flesh and will bring us to see Him face-to-face!

God has been at work because of His favor. His mercy creates an abundance and prosperity that are possible because He is the Creator and Sustainer and Redeemer of all. Thanks be to God!

CHAPTER 10

Seek Blessing

In so many ways, blessings are all we have ever known. Yes, life is hard. Yes, even insurmountable troubles come. Still, we are constantly surrounded by God's gracious gifts. And though God's people are no longer as visibly set apart as the Israelites were, God continues to give us His gifts and work His will for all creation. God still demonstrates that He is a God of blessing with repeated, ongoing demonstrations and verbal revelation.

Wherever He is favorably present, people receive blessing. He speaks, though not all listen. He provides Bread from heaven, but people still grumble. Even the resurrection of the dead will not convince those who will not listen to Moses and the Prophets (Luke 16:31).

We may not be Abraham or Isaac, but God continues to send His Word and His servants to bring us His blessing and His saving gifts. We receive hope in Him as we hear His steadfast Word, grounding us in the acts of His Son and nothing besides His provision. God turns and makes His face to shine upon us, is gracious to us, and gives us the peace that passes all understanding.

But how do we seek the Lord's blessing? Are there steps we follow and paths we tread? There are occasions and tasks that are blessed within vocation, but what about seeking the Lord's favor in more than family and economics? How do we seek the characteristic of God's favor?

Berakah is a noun form of *brk* that means *gift* (although it is frequently still translated as "blessing"). It reminds us that blessings are freely given, never coerced. Stated another way, blessings are never an obligation: God owes His favor to no one. At the same time, Scripture clearly encourages us to seek His favor. God *wants* to turn to us in love and mercy.

It is not silly to seek blessing. It is not superstitious. It is not self-centered, as though God's blessings are limited—no personal request can divine His infinite love. Seeking God's blessing simply seeks the favorable attention of the God we love.

Of course, the best and most necessary way to seek God's favor is through forgiveness in His Son. This worship is the highest worship of Christ: to seek forgiveness of sins from Jesus is to truly acknowledge the Messiah.[1]

Wisdom Literature

The Bible's Wisdom Literature (Job, portions of the Psalms, Proverbs, Ecclesiastes, and Song of Solomon) reveals that broadly embracing God's teaching, and by it God, is also rewarded with blessing. The aphorisms—sayings and observations—predict God will bless (or curse) people based on His previous revelations. Their purpose is to persuade people individually to obey God and actively practice Torah piety.

Torah piety is a many-layered concept. It includes cherishing God's Word and living according to His revelation. *Torah* itself has a dual meaning, referring to God's teaching in general and the first five books of the Bible in particular.

Proverbs 3:33 summarizes the entire message of the Wisdom Literature regarding blessing:

> The Lord's curse is on the house of the wicked,
> but He blesses the dwelling of the righteous.

Righteous means "right with God." It is not a matter of external obedience, but of a God who provides His way of life amid countless paths to death.

In the Wisdom texts, God's attitude is pictured as directly affecting reality. God blesses the home of the righteous as a constant condition. General prosperity and success accompany his undertakings, because of God's favorable disposition toward him.

God's attitude toward a person is pictured as directly and continually influencing that person's fate. Blessing and curse result from

God's attitude toward the person. God looks with scorn and disfavor upon the wicked, and so ruin and corruption follow them.

In the Wisdom Literature, prerequisites for blessing are at times one's relation to God (Psalms 112:1–2; 128:4; Proverbs 28:20) and at other times one's relation to other people (Proverbs 11:26; 22:9; 24:25). Rather than being mutually exclusive, one's relationship to God determines one's conduct toward others.

The content of blessing in the Wisdom aphorisms is usually not spelled out. When it is, it often consists of general things such as prosperity, children, good crops, and esteem.[2]

The Wisdom Literature also addresses that the wicked can prosper too. Yet, only God's blessing gives *lasting* wealth. Goods acquired by dishonest means, or simply by one's own labors without God's sanction, are fleeting (as in Psalm 127:1; Proverbs 20:21; 21:5; 28:20, 22).

Psalm 24:3 asks, "Who will ascend Yahweh's mountain? Who will stand in His holy place?" (CM). Verses 4–5 answer: the person who has clean hands and a pure heart, who has no desire for what is false (deceit and idols). Jesus ascends the Lord's mountain. Christ stands in His holy place. He offers Himself to us as the way, the truth, and the life (John 14:6).

We seek God and His approval as we flee from sin and strive to do good. We seek Him in His teaching. We seek Him and His blessing in His Word and His gifts of life: Baptism, Absolution, and the Lord's Supper. We seek Him in prayer.

Prayer

In ancient times, people prayed out loud. Quiet prayers were rare and rather odd—consider the priest's reaction when Hannah prayed and moved only her lips (1 Samuel 1:12–15). This gives us a privileged position to consider the role of prayer in the Old Testament, particularly as it pertains to blessing.

When people prayed for God to bless, their prayer did more than make a request. Prayed out loud, the prayer affected those within hearing distance. Such prayers, including our instinctive "God bless you!"

could comfort, reassure, remind, or instruct the person for whom the prayer is uttered.

In the Old Testament, prayers served a wide variety of functions as man blesses man through prayer. In Genesis 28:3–4, Isaac uses prayer as individual instruction and persuasion: Jacob was not to seek a Canaanite wife (Genesis 28:6). In Deuteronomy 26:15, the prayer unites the Israelite community to call upon God to fulfill His covenantal promises in remembrance of their covenant. Both 2 Samuel 7:29 and 1 Chronicles 17:27 function as audible amens, and when Moses uttered a prayer in Deuteronomy 1:11, it was to avoid misunderstanding among the people!

Praying aloud can do the following:

- Remind
- Comfort
- Assure
- Instruct
- Encourage

Of course, other prayers simply asked for personal benefits. For example, the Chronicler inserted an anecdote into a genealogy regarding Jabez. In 1 Chronicles 4:10, Jabez cries out to God:

> "Oh that You would bless me and enlarge my border, and that Your hand might be with me, and that You would keep me from harm so that it might not bring me pain!" And God granted what he asked.

This is included in Scripture to show that God listens to prayer and that we may freely ask for great things. No promise is attached that we will automatically get them, but we may freely ask mighty things of the almighty God (Isaiah 7:10–13). At the same time, God cannot turn in favor toward that which He disdains.

When God answers prayer, He abides by His Word.

God has revealed that He desires to work in certain ways. It is His will to save only through His Son. He desires that all nations be blessed through Abraham's blessing, resting in God's steadfast care and trusting His Word. And so we pray that all will thank and praise Jesus as the Savior of the world and that His will be done on earth as it is in heaven.

God also likes to be asked. The Father knows what we need before we ask Him, yet He teaches us to pray (Matthew 6:8–13). In humility, we are not to be anxious, saying, "What shall we eat?" but we are to seek first the kingdom of God and His righteousness (Matthew 6:31, 33).

In His kingdom, God takes our sins and problems upon Himself so that His blessings can truly be ours. God is the giver of every good and perfect gift (James 1:17), and as Luther, writing about the Second Article, so graphically describes: "We see how He has completely poured forth Himself [Matthew 26:28] and withheld nothing from us [2 Corinthians 8:9]."[3]

Unsought Blessing

Yet, the fact remains that fallen man struggles against being the blessed. We want to be the one to establish right, wrong, and all the rules. We want to be the actors rather than passive receivers. We want success. We want to determine our own sacrifices. We want to save the world!

Many blessings have become so taken for granted that society scorns them. Few want fertility; most crave control. Old age is hidden, and gray hair is unrecognized as the crown of glory it is (Proverbs 16:31). Produce is passed by as "junk food" is endeared. We want comforts strictly apart from needing to be comforted, and everyone wants to be favored, but few desire the favor of God.

Times are coming when our current ways of life may change. How will we handle the terrible things in the world when they come even closer? Christians killed, women and children sold into sex trade, starvation, and unspeakable evils? What will that mean in terms of whether we are still blessed? How will we speak about God's blessing?

Blessing is not the opposite of suffering. Deuteronomy 2:7 describes God's care of the Israelites during the wilderness wanderings:

> For the LORD your God has blessed you in all the work of your hands. He knows your going through this great wilderness. These forty years the LORD your God has been with you. You have lacked nothing.

God knew their hardships and remained with them. He knows ours as well and abides with us. We may still seek the Lord where He is found (Isaiah 55:6): "Blessed be the Lord, who daily bears us up; God is our salvation" (Psalm 68:19).

Jesus enters our lives and our needs. He reveals that blessings are a mercy rather than a visible merit, a salve at times rather than the fullness of salvation. And, though blessings can be rewards, they are entirely a creation of our infinite God, who has already saved us.

Jesus remains central. Distractions away from Him are no longer blessings but temptations.

Looks can be deceiving, but the Word of God is not. Blessings aren't always easy: "Many are the afflictions of the righteous, but the LORD delivers him out of them all" (Psalm 34:19). They aren't always without suffering, waiting, and great tedium.

What can we say?

- The blessed can suffer: Jesus did.
- Looks can be deceiving, but God's favor revolves around Jesus.
- Blessings are a mercy, not an escape.
- Our Lord delivers us from our needs in Jesus, and when Christ comes again, He will deliver us from all our struggles.
- Just as we pray for daily bread, the Lord *daily* bears us up.
- God abides with us, remaining with us through our hardships.

Seek the Lord and His blessing in His Word. It takes God's Word to reveal God's blessings. And, as a sign of His favor, no earthly blessing is intended to be a distraction from God's greatest gift: His Son. Rather, as we bear our crosses and sacrifice in love for our neighbor, we follow Him and abide in His teaching.

Jeremiah is a perfect antidote against misconceptions about blessings. His first book of prophecies includes this beloved line: "For I know the plans I have for you, declares the LORD, plans for welfare and not for evil, to give you a future and a hope" (Jeremiah 29:11). These words were written to the grieving survivors in the Babylonian exile. That divine plan tied together the effects of continually breaking the conditional covenant with the unconditional Abrahamic Blessing. There would be a future and a hope, but also an extensive, hard, seventy-year exile.

What does the Lord say through Jeremiah about blessings and woes?

Thus says the LORD:

"Cursed is the man who trusts in man
  and makes flesh his strength,
  whose heart turns away from the LORD.
He is like a shrub in the desert,
  and shall not see any good come.
He shall dwell in the parched places of the wilderness,
  in an uninhabited salt land.
"Blessed is the man who trusts in the LORD,
  whose trust is the LORD.
He is like a tree planted by water,
  that sends out its roots by the stream,
and does not fear when heat comes,
  for its leaves remain green,
and is not anxious in the year of drought,
for it does not cease to bear fruit." (Jeremiah 17:5–8)

Who will water us if not the Lord? "If anyone thirsts, let him come to Me and drink. Whoever believes in Me, as the Scripture has said, 'Out of his heart will flow rivers of living water' " (John 7:37b–38). Where is our stream, the physical location associated with blessing? Our congregation.

Things are not right with the world, but we may still seek God where He may be found. We may receive God's favor in His Word and the gifts given to His Church.

CHAPTER 11

Receive Blessing

A psalmist writes, "Blessed is He who comes in the name of the LORD! We bless you from the house of the LORD" (Psalm 118:26). Christ is blessed indeed, alleluia! He is the highest of all high priests, the Davidic King, and the Messiah, who ushers in the Age of Blessing! And we gather in congregations to receive His inheritance and His eternal blessing, including the forgiveness of sins and life everlasting.

The Divine Service both reflects and shares God's blessings. It speaks God's Word directly to us and gathers us in the name of God. It offers the union of God's Word and creation, both in the Sacraments and our resurrection.

> The Divine Service is a rich reflection and source of God's blessing.

Divine Service

Church is one of the only places where we are primarily receivers and passive. It is a place of provision under a single, benevolent Father and a brotherhood by incorporation into Christ.

The Divine Service is built around God's revelation of Himself and how He comes to His people in favor through the blessing of His Son. Blessings are throughout, including six traditional blessings:

1. "The Lord be with you."
2. "Grace and peace to you from God our Father and the Lord Jesus Christ."
3. "The peace of God, which passes all understanding, keep your hearts and minds in Christ Jesus."

4. "The peace of the Lord be with you always."
5. A blessing in dismissal following reception of the Lord's Supper.
6. The final Benediction, often either Aaronic or Pauline.

Throughout the service, we draw upon Old and New Testament blessings. We confess our sins, because God blesses us with forgiveness in His Son. We cry out, "Kyrie," because our God blesses us with His mercy. We use our voices in praise and thanksgiving to the God of the life-giving Word.

Pastors are positioned, according to their vocation, to bless their flock. In the stead and by the command of Christ, the ordained are called to incorporate us into Christ and His blessings by Word and deed. By speaking God's promises—and aren't all God's promises blessings?—he speaks every promise as a benediction of blessing.[1]

Within the sermon, the pastor blesses us with God's Word, but not in any generic sense. He proclaims the promises of God and enlivens with the Gospel. Like Moses, he personally delivers both Law and Gospel: God's commands and His mercy for the sake of Christ.

Within the congregation, our gracious Lord blesses us with food and drink, brothers and sisters, and news of a vast harvest field. He promises the longevity of eternal life! Not because of our obedience or merit, but because Jesus is the way, the truth, and the life.

In the house of our Father, we walk in the ways of our spiritual forefathers. We approach because He has shown previous mercy. We ask for forgiveness so that He will continue to dwell among us. We pray for God's protection and deliverance. We live and thrive only because of Him and His mercy promised to men of old.

As our God is the God of the living, we join together with all the people of God, even Abraham and Moses. We pray. We ponder and benefit from God's performative Word, receiving the abundant gifts of His favor, even forgiveness of sins, life, and salvation. We enter into the very name of God in Baptism, and we prosper with the Bread from heaven in the Lord's Supper. We receive Priestly Blessings and, in thanks to God, return blessings to Him.

Blessing the Lord

To be honest, people can get carried away with the idea of blessing the Lord. We do not elevate Him. We certainly share from the gifts He has given us, but we do not add to His storehouse of blessing (Malachi 3:10). He is God entirely apart from us.

Basically, the early use of *baruk* to thank or praise men expanded to also thank and praise God. Depending on the recipient, the Hebrew term is translated as "blessed" or "praised." This is a common linguistic phenomenon.

Bless the Lord = to give Him thanks and praise

Many of the passages employing *brk* contain spontaneous expressions of praise uttered by people in response to a specific act of God in the course of everyday life. Such praise could be part of an act of worship (Genesis 24:26–27, 48; Exodus 18:10–12), just as we continue to use songs of King David, Mary, Zechariah, and so on.

Praise expressions with *brk* have much to teach us. Practically all related contexts describe the reason for praise as either a prior act by God or, if the praise is doxological, as a trait of God. This shapes our understanding of praise by emphasizing that God is praised because He has *already* blessed the people, rather than to elicit blessing.

Thankfulness and praise as described in the *brk* praise passages does not seek inward assurance or emotional pleasure. It stands on the already accomplished, steadfast loving kindness and mercy of God. Such an understanding of God's prior saving work—whether that is the exodus and conquest or Christ's incarnation, death, and resurrection—allows us to trust Christ and His trustworthy objective signs rather than seek subjective signs that could mislead.

The Psalms portray praise as man's duty to God. Our Lord has no needs, yet He can delight in His creation and their actions. Our thankful praise, then, is how we repay God for His goodness to us.

Yet, God is not the only one who benefits. Praise has both an illocutionary and a perlocutionary force, and both forces are present in all forms of praise employing *brk* in the Old Testament. Praising God both addresses God (illocutionary) and others (perlocutionary), encouraging them to join in His most worthy praise:

> Thank the Lord and sing His praise; tell ev'ryone what He has done. Let all who seek the Lord rejoice and proudly bear His name. He recalls His promises and leads His people forth in joy with shouts of thanksgiving. Alleluia, alleluia![2]

Note the centrality of God's action, the prominence of promise, the inclusive audience, and His sharable name. *Alleluia* translates as *Praise Yah/Yahweh, you people.* The canticle revolves around God's blessings and His character as the blesser.

"Blessed is He who comes in the name of the Lord!" In Jesus, we see both the infinite blesser and the infinitely blessed. We praise Him, who both gives and receives for our sake, taking our sins upon Himself to give us His righteousness. And, "What shall I render to the Lord for all His benefits to me?"

> I will offer the sacrifice of thanksgiving and will call on the name of the Lord. I will take the cup of salvation and will call on the name of the Lord. I will pay my vows to the Lord now in the presence of all His people, in the courts of the Lord's house, in the midst of you, O Jerusalem.[3]

Of course, we all experience more than thankfulness in this life. Praise does not encompass all of Israel's faith nor ours. God's Word includes powerful laments and brokenhearted cries. There are long recitals of God's saving acts and exhortations to follow the Law. There are many examples of falling away and of repentance by the Spirit.

But blessing is not set apart from our times of mourning, discouragement, or other need. God takes it upon Himself to enter our lives by His Word and Spirit. He blesses before we praise, even as He gives us life before we seek it.

Do blessings affect days and weeks, relationships and scenarios? Yes, but not by blocking out all sorrow or pulling the strings of a puppet. God's choices and His answers to our prayers may remain hidden or be revealed at a much later time.

The Priestly Blessing

We close with one of the most common and famous blessings: the Priestly, or Aaronic, Blessing.

> The LORD bless you and keep you;
> the LORD make His face to shine upon you and be
> gracious to you;
> the LORD lift up His countenance upon you and give
> you peace. (Numbers 6:24–26)

This benediction—in a liturgical sense, *the* Benediction—shows more clearly than any other passage how God's blessing is intimately connected to His favorable attitude. Invoking the blessing calls upon God to have an *attitude* of goodwill toward the persons blessed.

All three verses commence with a general expression of God's favor and end with a request for a somewhat more concrete benefit. The initial phrase is the most general: it is an all-inclusive type of petition. In the next, God making His face shine on someone denotes God displaying His favor (*hesed*) and attention toward him by acting on His behalf (Psalm 31:16; 80:3, 7, 19, where God delivers persons from distress).[4] The third refers back to previous lines, almost referencing a smile, with peace dependent upon God's keeping.

Numbers 6:27 describes the effect the Benediction will have: "They shall put My name upon the people of Israel, and I will bless them." As Christians, we continue to use this blessing in confidence because God has placed His name upon us through Baptism. He has made us spiritual heirs of Israel and even joined us with His sole heir, Jesus Christ.

God is pictured as complying voluntarily with the requests of the Benediction. Yet, circumstances matter. To be effective within Old Testament times, the Benediction must be uttered by the priests, who mediate for God, and in the correct form. The context implies, and actual practice confirms, that the Benediction was spoken only on important religious occasions to assure the people that God is indeed favorably disposed toward them and will continue to bless them.

The priests of old were authorized to bless the people, and now pastors, too, bless those under their pastoral care. They put the name of God on His people. They set the Lord's Table. They tend the flock that the Lord prospers. They are to visit the sick and tend the guilty or shamed with the favor of God, who sees them in their need.

God Blessing Man

- Through His attitude and attention
- Through creation
- Through mediation
- Through His Word and Sacraments

Because our God is the triune God, we can consider the blessings in the three parts of the creeds: the Father's created and sustaining gifts, the Son's salvific work, and the Spirit's call through the Gospel into the communion of saints, forgiveness of sins, resurrection of the body, and the life everlasting. Altogether, as revealed by Scripture, they are gifts of gracious, unearned blessing, upholding the incarnation and the new creation to come, expressing the totality of God's favor.

The Father continues to knit life and send rain. He sends us His Son, the Bread of heaven, as well as our daily bread. Christ, as our Mediator, intercedes for us with God the Father and brings us God's forgiveness, favor, and blessing. And, as Christ continues to send us His emissaries and servants, the Holy Spirit keeps us in His Word that we may trust His promises.

The apostle Paul recognized that he bore blessing from God for the sake of the people. He wrote, "I know that when I come to you I will come in the fullness of the blessing of Christ" (Romans 15:29). He, like our pastors today, brought people the entirety of God's blessing in Christ and the Gospel. In vocation, we bless one another, sharing the gifts God has given us according to our relationships and opportunities.

Though we are apt to stray, God offers us His most holy favor through His Son, our Savior. He gives us both His Word and physical gifts tied to His Word: the Sacraments of Baptism and the Lord's Supper. These tie together washing and eating with faith, forgiveness, and assurance in the accomplishments of our God.

As God continues to create new hearts, even in dark times, we may give thanks for our daily bread, whether it is a lot or a little. We may ask His blessing that His creation may thrive. We can embrace life despite the costs, growing pains, and struggles of longevity. We can live in thankfulness and praise as we live by faith and not by sight.

God's Word raises up people for Himself and creation, and He sends His Word that our infinite God may grant infinite blessing. Blessed be God, indeed, who withholds nothing from those who walk in His ways (Psalm 84:11)! He comes to us with blessing through a virgin's womb and a Father's love, by His promise and benediction, in good times and in bad, and death shall never part us. May God look upon us and all nations with His favor and give us His peace. Amen.

Selective Bibliography

Kleinig, John. *Leviticus.* Concordia Commentary. St. Louis: Concordia Publishing House, 2004.

Kleinig, John. "Pastoring by Blessing," *Lutheran Theological Journal,* 43/1. Adelaide: Australian Lutheran College, 2009. Online at www.johnkleinig.com/files /5513/5934/3089 /Pastoring_by_Blessing.pdf.

Luther, Martin. Luther's Works. American Edition, vol. 41: *Church and Ministry III.* Minneapolis: Augsburg Fortress Press, 1966.

Lutheran Service Book. St. Louis: Concordia Publishing House, 2006.

McCain, Paul, ed. *Concordia: The Lutheran Confessions: A Reader's Edition of the Book of Concord.* St. Louis: Concordia Publishing House, 2006.

Mitchell, Christopher. *The Meaning of* BRK *"To Bless" in the Old Testament.* Atlanta: Scholars Press and the Society of Biblical Literature, 1987.

Speiser, E. A. "I Know Not the Day of My Death. *Journal of Biblical Literature,* 74:254.

Wilson, Robert. *Prophecy and Society in Ancient Israel.* Philadelphia: Fortress Press, 1980.

Wood, Bryant. "Great Discoveries in Biblical Archaeology: The Nuzi Tablets," *Bible and Spade,* Winter 2005 issue. Online at www.biblearchaeology.org/post/2006/02/27/Great-Discoveries-in-Biblical-Archaeology-The-Nuzi-Tablets.aspx#Article.

Notes

Introduction

1. James Reston Jr., *Luther's Fortress: Martin Luther and His Reformation Under Siege* (New York: Basic Books, 2015), 141.

Chapter 1

1. We may be more familiar with psalms of praise than psalms of lament or anguish, but there are many psalms for the downtrodden. By all means, pray those psalms! They include Psalms 6; 7; 13; 22; 28; 31; 35; 38; 40; 44; 53; 55; 56; 69; 74; 77; 79; 80; 86; 88; 89; 102; 109; 142!

Chapter 2

1. *The Christian Cyclopedia,* edited by Erwin Lueker, is available online at cyclopedia.lcms.org.
2. Luther's Small Catechism, explanation of the First Article.

Chapter 3

1. Formula of Concord Solid Declaration VII 76.
2. Martin Luther, "The Estate of Marriage, 1522," *Luther's Works,* vol. 45, ed. Walther I Brandt (Philadelphia: Fortress, 1962), 18.
3. Also see 1 Samuel 9:13, where *brk* Piel denotes consecration by a person.

Chapter 4

1. Though the noun could denote a recipient of blessing (as in Ezekiel 34:26; Psalm 37:26; Proverbs 10:7), or as a proverbial example of a blessed person (as in Zechariah 8:13; cf. Genesis 48:20), the most suitable meaning here is "source of blessing" (as in Isaiah 19:24).
2. God promises the status of being such a mediator in Genesis 12:3; 18:17–18; 22:18; 26:4; 28:14.
3. There is a middle meaning in the result clauses in Genesis 18:18; 22:18; 26:4; 28:14. For our purposes, consider the following:

   Passive: be blessed

   Reflexive: bless oneself/invoke blessing for oneself

Reciprocal: bless each other

Middle: acquire blessing (for oneself)

4. *LSB*, Divine Service, Setting Three, Nunc Dimittis, pp. 199–200.
5. The compound name El Elyon is found in Genesis 14:18–20 and Psalm 78:35: "They remembered that God [Elohim] was their rock, the Most High God [El Elyon] their redeemer." The parallel indicates they, El and Elyon, are the same, though described slightly differently. Elyon stands alone as a name in Numbers 24:16; Deuteronomy 32:8; Isaiah 14:13–14; 2 Samuel 22:14, which firmly identifies him as Yahweh; and Psalm 97:9.
6. Three verses in addition to Genesis 14:19 employ the Piel of *brk* to speak a benediction of praise or congratulations. In Joshua 14:13, Joshua blessed Caleb when he gave him the territory around Hebron as an inheritance. In 2 Samuel 8:10 and 1 Chronicles 18:10, congratulations are expressed.
7. In 2 Kings 18:31 = Isaiah 36:16–17, Sennacherib's field commander invites the people of Jerusalem to surrender: 'Make a treaty (*berakah*) with me, and come out to me, so each one of you can eat from his vine and fig tree . . . until I come and take you to a land like your land" (CM). This blessing either expresses hope for peaceful, friendly relations, or it could be interpreted to mean a state in which both parties bless each other, i.e., work for the benefit of each other, at least in theory. The noun stands for the blessing clauses of a vassal treaty.

The meaning in 2 Kings 18:31 = Isaiah 36:18 is quite similar to its meaning in Deuteronomy 11:26–29; 30:1, 19; Joshua 8:34, where the word pair stands for the Sinai covenant. Vassal treaties, like the Sinai covenant, normally concluded with invocations of the gods to bless or curse the vassal depending on his obedience.

8. For other examples, see Deuteronomy 33:20; 1 Samuel 25:32–33; 1 Kings 5:7 = 2 Chronicles 2:12; 1 Kings 10:8–9 = 2 Chronicles 9:8.

Chapter 5

1. Bryant Wood, "Great Discoveries in Biblical Archaeology: The Nuzi Tablets," *Bible and Spade*, Winter 2005. Online at http://www.biblearchaeology.org/post/2006/02/27/Great-Discoveries-in-Biblical-Archaeology-The-Nuzi-Tablets.aspx#Article.
2. For example, the Nuzi tablets include documents showing husbands adopting wives as sisters in order to grant the wife greater protection and a higher legal status. Such historical documents help shed light on Scripture passages such as Genesis 12:10–20 and chapters 20 and 26.

3. E. A. Speiser, "I Know Not the Day of My Death," *Journal of Biblical Literature*, 74:254.

Chapter 6

1. Martin Luther describes the marks of the Church to be (1) the Word of God preached, believed, professed, and lived; (2) Baptism taught, believed, and administered; (3) the Sacrament of the Altar rightly administered, believed, and received, according to Christ's institution; (4) the Office of the Keys exercised publicly for the forgiveness of sins; (5) the calling, consecrating, and ordaining of ministers—preachers and hearers; (6) prayer, public praise, and thanksgiving to God; and (7) the sacred cross, including misfortune and persecution. See Part III of *On Councils and the Church* to read more on the topic of the seven marks of the Church by which it can be recognized.
2. AE 41:164–65.
3. *ahab* (Deuteronomy 7:13; 23:5); *ḥanan* (Numbers 6:25; Psalm 67:1); *ḥesed* (Deuteronomy 7:12); *ratsah* (Deuteronomy 33:11, 24); and *ratṣon* (Deuteronomy 33:16, 23).

Chapter 7

1. This would include the teachings of Exodus 20–24, the Book of Leviticus, and the Book of Numbers.
2. For further reading, consider Dr. John Kleinig, *Leviticus*, Concordia Commentary, pp. 576ff.
3. Similarly, Deuteronomy 28:12.
4. The Canaanites knew that the Lord had promised to give the Israelites the land. They had prior warning about the military prowess. They knew that the Lord God was not constrained as their own gods (Joshua 2:9–11). Still, they would not follow Him.
5. Deuteronomy 15:14 is typical: when an Israelite slave is set free, "You must generously give to him from your flocks, threshing floor, and wine vat. You should give to him that which Yahweh will have blessed you with" (CM; similarly, Deuteronomy 12:7; 14:24; 16:10). Likewise, the Israelites are told that when they slaughter animals they can eat as much as they want, "according to the blessing which your God Yahweh will have given you" (Deuteronomy 12:15; similarly, 16:17).
6. Luther's Small Catechism, Daily Prayers, Asking a Blessing.

Chapter 8

1. Pual is similar to Piel, except that Pual is passive—the subject receives the action of the verb.
2. See Robert Wilson, *Prophecy and Society in Ancient Israel* (Philadelphia: Fortress Press, 1980), pp. 132–33.
3. Zion is often used as a synonym for Jerusalem.
4. Though dew is a blessing mentioned elsewhere, including Genesis 27:28; Deuteronomy 33:28; and Zechariah 8:12, dew is not connected with fertility here and so is likely not alluding to the other passages.
5. The Hithpael of *brk* in verse 2 with *goyim* as the subject and *bo'*, "by means of/through him," is an allusion to the five Patriarchal Promises of blessing for all through the mediation of Abraham and his Seed.

Chapter 9

1. John Kleinig, "Pastoring by Blessing," *Lutheran Theological Journal*, 43/1 (2009). On page 3 as found here: www.johnkleinig.com/files/5513/5934/3089/Pastoring_by_Blessing.pdf.

Chapter 10

1. Apology of the Augsburg Confession V (III) 33.
2. In Psalm 5:11–12, the psalmist expresses his confidence that, because of God's favor toward him, God will bless him with protection from his enemies. Psalm 128 describes the benefits of those who fear the Lord (vv. 1, 4): they eat what they have labored for (v. 2) and have a fruitful wife with children (v. 3). The phrase in verse 2a denotes general prosperity, while verse 4 describes these benefits as blessings: "For that is how a man who fears Yahweh is blessed" (CM). Like the Prophetic Apocryphal Blessings, external stated blessings can serve symbolically.
3. Large Catechism II 26.

Chapter 11

1. John Kleinig, "Pastoring by Blessing," *Lutheran Theological Journal*, 43/1 (Adelaide: Australian Lutheran College, 2009).
2. *LSB*, Divine Service, Setting One, Post-Communion Canticle, p. 164. See Psalm 105:1–3, 42–43; 1 Chronicles 16:8–10.
3. *LSB*, Divine Service, Settings One and Two, pp. 159–160, 176, based on Psalm 116:12–13, 17–19.

4. In Psalm 44:3, the light of God's face denotes the aid God gives to His people because He is favorably disposed toward them. God lifting up His face toward someone is equivalent to making His face shine on someone (cf. Psalm 4:6). It denotes God giving His favorable attention to someone. Contrast that with God hiding His face out of anger, signifying that He withdraws His favor (Deuteronomy 31:17–18, 20).